QUESTIONING
GYPSY IDENTITY

QUESTIONING GYPSY IDENTITY

Ethnic Narratives in Britain and America

Brian A. Belton

A Division of Rowman & Littlefield Publishers, Inc.
Walnut Creek • Lanham • New York • Toronto • Oxford

ALTAMIRA PRESS
A division of Rowman & Littlefield Publishers, Inc.
1630 North Main Street, #367
Walnut Creek, CA 94596
www.altamirapress.com

Rowman & Littlefield Publishers, Inc.
A wholly owned subsidiary of
The Rowman & Littlefield Publishing Group, Inc.
4501 Forbes Boulevard, Suite 200
Lanham, MD 20706

PO Box 317
Oxford
OX2 9RU, UK

Copyright © 2005 by AltaMira Press

All rights reserved. No part of this publication may be reproduced, stored in a retrieval system, or transmitted in any form or by any means, electronic, mechanical, photocopying, recording, or otherwise, without the prior permission of the publisher.

British Library Cataloguing in Publication Information Available

Library of Congress Cataloging-in-Publication Data

Belton, Brian.
  Questioning Gypsy identity : ethnic narratives in Britain and America / Brian A. Belton.
    p. cm.
  Includes bibliographical references and index.
  ISBN 0-7591-0532-4 (alk. paper) — ISBN 0-7591-0533-2 (pbk. : alk. paper)
  1. Romanies—Ethnic identity. 2. Romanies—Great Britain.
  3. Romanies—United States. I. Title.

DX115.B36 2004
305.891'497041—dc22

2004015622

Printed in the United States of America

∞™ The paper used in this publication meets the minimum requirements of American National Standard for Information Sciences—Permanence of Paper for Printed Library Materials, ANSI/NISO Z39.48-1992.

To Mum and Dad

Contents

1	Introduction: A Gypsy Lineage	1
2	The Ethnic Gypsy	13
3	Defining American Gypsies	39
4	Historical Genesis of American Gypsies	69
5	Gypsies in Social Bondage	93
6	Ethnicity as Narrative	111
7	Colonialism and the Gypsies	135
8	Defining Legislation	147
9	Toward a New Paradigm of Gypsy Identity	169
Appendix: The Gypsy Lore Society (GLS)		187
Bibliography		189
Index		199
About the Author		000

1

Introduction: A Gypsy Lineage

Jimmy Stone was a Gypsy whose family took up residence on Bonny Downs, a tolerated site in Barking that was, in the mid- and late nineteenth century, a parish in the southeastern English county of Essex. In 1914, the Gypsy boys from the site were recruited to serve King and country as a group, similar to the street recruitment of housed civilians throughout Britain. Jimmy, along with many of the men and boys from Bonny Downs, never returned to England. He was killed in 1916. All that came back to Catherine, his wife, was a blood-stained greeting card embroidered with flowers.

Catherine then had to look for some way to support her three young children, Celia, Eleanor, and Jim. Like many women of her class at this time, she was obliged to find a husband. She bore another child, Clara, by her second husband, who was also lost to the battlefields of Europe. After the war, Catherine married a widowed seaman, Bill Battles, to whom she bore Doris and Vera. Bill brought his only child, Mary, to the family and was to spend much of his life after leaving the sea in the "Ship and Shovel" public house in Barking.

Young Jim Stone, after playing a part in the liberation of Europe, including a number of concentration camps, became a toolmaker. Eleanor married a man from the tough East London industrial area of Canning Town. James Edward Belton was a stoker in the Gas Works at Beckton, a mile or so from his family home. James saw active service throughout World War II as a Royal Engineer and was one of the many who freed Norway from Axis control. In the early 1950s, alongside his son, James Jr., he set up a number of small businesses that prospered during the 1960s and early 1970s.

Before going bankrupt, the consequence of drug- and gambling-related problems, James Jr. married Joyce, the daughter of a Poplar fireman who was also an active local socialist politician. Young Jim and Joyce had two sons. The extended family followed many of what are often thought of as East End and Gypsy traditions: hop picking, collecting china, and annual visits to a regional horse fair set deep in England's garden county of Kent. Eleanor died in the mid-1980s, about ten years after her husband. Like her sister and her mother, she was a victim of asbestosis, contracted from the notorious asbestos factory that prospered and poisoned the West Essex-East London border area of Barking. Eleanor had spent her girlhood working and frolicking, as if in sand, with other youngsters during lunch and tea times in the great banks of raw asbestos dust that were stored in the factory.

Having given up self-employment after the death of his father, James Jr. retired from his job as a local authority dog handler in the late 1980s. His eldest son, after studying as a draughtsman, became a police officer. He married Susan, the daughter of a works foreman, employed at the massive dockside Tate and Lyall's sugar refinery in Silver Town, East London. Young James and Susan had three children. One daughter became a teacher, the other worked in the city, and the youngest child, the son, another Jimmy, delved into the performing arts. Jim and Joyce's younger son, during a dynamic career as a member of West Ham United Football Club's roving army of adolescent storm troopers of the early 1970s and a string of jobs, took up working with young people. This brought him to Canada for a time, from where he traveled to the United States, spending a year making a precarious living from the greyhound tracks of the southern states. Returning to Britain and following professional training, he became a youth worker, then gained master's and doctoral degrees while employed as a lecturer in higher education. He went on to write a novel and a string of books on a wide range of subjects. With Rosy, a former North London, arsenal-supporting, self-ascribed rag-a-muffin child of immigrants (Irish and Belgium) who is now a National Inspector of Further Education, he has a ten-year-old son who celebrates his East End, Gypsy, Gaelic, Flemish ancestry with a great deal of pride and humor, but whom people know simply as Christian, an eccentric, loving, sensitive, and intelligent little boy, a developing human being with a budding and interesting personality. He is intrigued by the world around him, his pet dog, Reg (a tubby and exuberant black Labrador), medieval history, the meaning of words, Warhammers, and the Simpsons. That is who he mostly and really is; *that* is *his* identity.

The huge maternal influence of Eleanor persists. The interior of the family home still looks like a caravan.

A Book about Gypsies and the Gypsy

This example of Gypsy lineage illustrates . . . the idea—often promulgated in the literature connected with groups variously called Rom, Romany, Gypsy, and Traveler (to mention just the most popular epithets given to current or formerly itinerant groups)—of an uninterrupted and unmediated consistency of blood or heritage, given the influences of modern existence, is somewhat limited. The background depicted above will be familiar to many who have been connected with Traveling and Gypsy lifestyles. This book brings together stories of Gypsy and Traveler life, elucidations of encounter and experience, with a range of theories relating to social interaction and process, and examines how identity arises out of the cultural complexity of individual biographies, families, communities, and the great blocks of people that we, as a society, categorize and label. Central to this task is an effort to explore and understand how Gypsy ethnicity is produced out of a particular type of social narrative. Overall, the collective analysis problematizes the conceptual basis of racial and ethnic categorization that portrays Gypsies as largely arising out of a biological nexus.

In this book, I argue that an ethnic and racial focus on Gypsies, portrayed as a distinct population within American and European society, has given rise to an ethnic narrative of Gypsy identity. This provides a less ambiguous and more informative explanation of the social nature of the Gypsy population than interpretations based on blood, breed, stock, ethnicity, or race that dominate the literature. The Gypsy population is described in the literature concerned with this group as consisting of a range of diverse groups but, at the same time, as being a collectivity that constitutes a people of a definite type. Within this paradigm, hereditary considerations predominate; Gypsies are depicted as the product of biological inheritance. This essentially ethnic and racially oriented analysis is not always overt; however, texts do make definite references to Gypsies as an ethnic group or race (see Hawes and Perez 1995; and Fraser 1992, for example). In the pages that follow, I argue that the Gypsy population in America has emerged out of the complexity of historical, social, and economic history. I will suggest that this group is made up of a melding of people from a diverse range of backgrounds and, as such, does not constitute an ethnic or racial whole; I question the description of this group as a homogenous collective, whether defined as Traveler, Rom, Romany, Gypsy, or other. At the same time, I will seek to address the lack of a contextual and social perspective in theory relating to Gypsies, exploring Gypsy identity and considering the part social influences play in the generation of this population. I will attempt to develop a more structured understanding of this identity.

In the first paragraphs of chapter 2, I propose that race, culture, and ethnicity have become interchangeable terms and that each of these tools of categorization is, at least in part, a social construct. This motivates a critical analysis of the notion of Gypsy ethnicity, which highlights the limitations of the literature that I argue fails to adequately consider the broader social context in which the Gypsy population exists.

Using biographical and narrative analysis, in chapter 2 I begin to develop what is the major theme of the book: that ethnicity in general and Gypsy ethnicity in particular are principally social constructions. While this position might be familiar to contemporary students of sociology and anthropology, it opposes the standard line of thought as expressed in the literature concerned with Gypsy identity, which overtly and covertly asserts the importance of inheritance and biology and a paradigm that promotes an understanding of Gypsy identity as the product of cultural transference through lineage. This, which might be understood as ethnic reductionism, is not easily distinguishable from a racial categorization.

In the second part of chapter 2, I suggest that theories and descriptions of Gypsy ethnicity have been articulated on a foundation of a range of abstract assumptions relating to what are depicted in the literature focusing on Gypsies as the crucial ethnic and racial markers of Gypsy identity: romanticism, ideas about Gypsy language itinerancy, self-identification, ritual, and rite. I critique these claimed indicators of ethnicity and demonstrate that they are unreliable determinants of Gypsy identity and categorization. On the basis of this analysis, again using biographical material, I argue that in order to establish a clearer etiology of the Gypsy population a broader theoretical perspective needs to be developed that includes consideration of social and economic factors, moving beyond ethnic and cultural determinants.

Throughout chapter 3 the proposal, which is inherent in the literature focusing on Gypsy identity, that groups of people—variously labeled as Gypsies, Rom, Romany, Roma, and Travelers, among other epithets—constitute a homogenous population made up of heterogeneous elements—this commonality in shared difference that is formulated as the basis of Gypsy ethnicity—is critiqued and problematized. This involves an examination of the character of American Gypsy studies, which I demonstrate practically duplicates British and European analysis, and the questioning of other characterizations of Gypsy ethnicity as portrayed in the literature concerning itself with Gypsy issues. The limitations of this literature are discussed, including the lack of a satisfactory sociological perspective, which disallows any meaningful consideration of the effects of social structure and action on the Gypsy population.

The flaws of the tendency within the literature to represent Gypsy identity as essentially a racial or ethnic category are pointed out, this penchant being energized via a paradigm of romanticism that is, in part, sustained by often illogical self-ascription to Gypsy identity and fragile language connections with exotic ethnic or racial origins. I argue that out of this specious contrivance the biological, hereditary Gypsy is constructed. This short-circuits reflection on the social determinants of power in the development of Gypsy identity.

Chapter 3 is concluded by questioning the reason for seeking to identify and categorize Gypsies. Looking to the discussion in chapter 4, I highlight the lack of contemplation in the literature concerned with Gypsy identity as to how social considerations might bind the Gypsy population into a collective entity.

The historical background of American Gypsies as portrayed in literature is examined in chapter 4. This analysis encompasses a critique of the idea of a root or founding conduit of the American Gypsy population via penal transportation in the colonial period, and the subsequent immigration of the eighteenth, nineteenth, and twentieth centuries. I suggest that the migrating and transported individuals and groups, labeled before departure from Europe, whom much of the literature sees as the progenitors of the current Gypsy population, may not have, in reality, been ethnically, racially, or even socially Gypsies. I go on to examine the framework that attempts to rationalize a historical and current Gypsy presence in America, despite the assertion (Hancock 1987) that this presence is denied by Gypsies who, confusingly, are thought to have dissipated into the wider population of the United States to such an extent that they have become invisible (the claim seems to be that a view about the presence of a particular people has been attained through having made contact with those people, even through they are invisible!). I conclude chapter 4 by pointing out the contradictory nature of this position, the extremity of which brings the notion of the American Gypsy into question.

Chapter 5 looks at the adoption of weak forms of power (Hall 1991, 34) in the form of the embracing and acceptance of a Gypsy ethnic identity. I analyze how this affects the political and social position of Gypsies and helps maintain existing forms of domination and oppression. I examine how the resulting categorization enables the marketing of Gypsies by interested academics and professionals but at the same time risks potentially dangerous social consequences.

In the second part of chapter 5, continuing with the exploration of ethnicity as primarily a social construct, I suggest that ethnicity can be understood as a product of social closure (Weber 1922; Parkin 1979). I illustrate the potential role that access to social resources has in the creation of solidarity within excluded groups and how this might evolve into an ethnic definition and, as such, maintain and contribute to the generation of Gypsy ethnic identity

In chapter 6, I examine the nature of narrative and the ways in which life stories can tell us about the character of lives lived and how they are shaped in society. I discuss the power and nature of the ethnic narrative: how the stories of people's lives are products of social interaction.

This psychosocial perspective is premised on the ideas of symbolic interactionism (Mead 1934a), which highlights how the self and other selves interact to produce ethnic categories. Starting with an analysis of the constructs of symbolic interactionism (Sarbin 1986, 18), I examine ideas relating to narrative (Sutton-Smith 1986; Bruner 1987) and how this relates to the formation of ethnic identity. This demonstrates how stories about identity are adopted and ascribed, while illustrating the extent to which Gypsy identity (and ethnicity in general) is a product of social human interaction and not just a biological, racial, or ethnic phenomenon. However, I argue that a particular ethnic narrative of Gypsy identity dominates the understanding of the Gypsy population, a story of ethnic or biological difference.

In chapter 7, while exploring personal biography, I confirm the impact of narrative by deploying a Fanonian (Fanon 1952, 1961) perspective to develop the notion of a colonial narrative of Gypsy ethnicity that is produced by the interlocking and interaction of narratives. Within this, the Gypsy can tap into an ethnic affiliation that is seemingly political but is, in practice, based on taking on an identity as one of the oppressed. I argue that the resultant ethnic identity is forged not so much out of a fundamental feeling of ethnic unity, but as a response to the oppressor's definition and treatment of the Gypsy.

The Gypsy ethnic narrative links with the contention running through the literature pertaining to Gypsies (for example, see Fraser 1992) that this worldwide population has definite origins in or connections with the Indian subcontinent. I argue that ethnic narrative can be used to understand how ethnic identity or feelings of affiliation to an ethnicity can emerge from a shared social anxiety fostered by inequalities in the distribution of social resources. I propose that this association with an ethnic whole also meets sentimental and emotional needs connected to notions of belonging.

Continuing with the colonial simile, the last part of chapter 7 demonstrates how ethnic distinctions can be understood as the product of exploitative social and economic considerations (Kuper and Smith 1971). I highlight the resemblance between the social position of Gypsies and the colonized African pluralist societies. This once more shows that social and economic relations give rise to ethnicity-generating forces.

Alongside previous chapters, chapter 7 offers an alternative perspective, relative to the race arguments that characterize the literature relating to Gypsies and how Gypsy ethnicity and race is generated and maintained. I continue to argue that ethnicity is an idea rather than a definite carnal certainty and that Gypsy identity is the product of social action, a phenomenon that is engendered out of a collaboration of self with others. As such, it is possible to see ethnicity as a narrative thing. It is the ethnic narrative that exists rather than a concrete category. Thus, the meaning of ethnicity is made accessible and, as such, so are the reasons why ethnicity is used in the social realm.

In chapter 8, using Marxist and Foucauldian perspectives, I have argued that legislation affecting Gypsies both confirms and exacerbates the nature of society. I propose that forces inherent in the social fabric will amend or abolish processes and lifestyles that are counter to the social and economic practices that engender and support the social structure. I also call on Foucault's ideas relating to genealogy (Foucault 1972; McNay 1994) to demonstrate that the ethnic Gypsy arises out of power relations.

This analysis shows how the contemporary interpretations of Gypsy identity fail to withstand Foucauldian genealogical analysis. I suggest that ethnic categorization serves the control structures inherent in the workings of the capitalism. The colonial narrative, together with legislative marginalization, is consistent with and part of the whole panoply of discipline (Foucault 1977) that is premised, in terms of Gypsies, on the need to comply with social and market norms. This position highlights the partial treatment of legislative activity within the literature concerned with Gypsy affairs that portrays the policy that impacts on Gypsies as arising out of a general psychological disposition rather than being the product of the social environment (Hawes and Perez 1995, 17).

However, this legislation has a discernible linkage that is founded in the nature of the social formation of society and has both a limiting and disciplinary function. Out of this analysis arises a general conception of the meaning of Gypsy identity and the response to Gypsies. They are the other because they represent an alternative to market norms, departing as they do from social conventions that double as a means of observation and control, through known location and patterns of consumption and communication. Given this position, the prevalent argument in the literature—that the irrational psychological response of discrimination is the fundamental factor motivating the harassment and oppression of Gypsies—can be seen to be flawed. It lacks an appropriate analysis of the societal context within which Gypsies are defined as a category.

I also propose that the Gypsy has been generated as a deviant and as such is dispatched (formally or informally) to designated areas of control. This being the case, the laws impacting Gypsy ways of life together with the site (Gypsy encampment) might be seen as means of discipline that are appropriate to the capitalist social formation. Finally, I argue that within the current social situation categorization cannot be avoided.

The book concludes with a reconciliation of the social nature of the emergence and presence of a Gypsy identity and a plea for and suggestions relating to the development of a new paradigm of Gypsy identity. This is not a proposal that undermines the notion of an American Gypsy identity, but, rather, a proposition that we attempt to understand that the individuals and groups that make up this category have a wide social base.

The Sociological Tradition

In this book, I argue that Gypsy identity is created and maintained not only by tradition and hereditary but also by social and ideological factors that give rise to the ethnic narrative of Gypsy identity. As such, I have aligned with the traditions of Göttingen University that began in the mid-eighteenth century, in that I examine the interconnectedness of Gypsy identity, relating it to and setting it within the social and economic processes of the contemporary era, in what might be understood as an exploration of the dynamics of antecedent events. This approach mirrors the method favored by Montesquieu: the analysis of the material and cultural environment and human interaction with the surroundings (Willems 1997, 36). I also stay true to a sociological heritage exemplified in the Chicago school tradition of social and cultural research.

The overall analysis contained in this book promotes an understanding of Gypsies, emphasizing the constant growth and the dynamism of this group. The work is an effort to develop an awareness of the intricate development of social, racial, and ethnic categorization and provide a broader understanding of the makeup and social constitution of the Gypsy population. The book also establishes a social meaning of ethnicity with regard to the Gypsy population through a critical examination of social, political, and cultural forces that create the ethnic narrative that is Gypsy identity.

An Outside Insider

The pages that follow are written from the perspective of one who has been an outsider and a spectator of Gypsies in America and the way this group is understood and responded to in this context. But I am, at the same time, an insider, having been raised with a clear knowledge of my own background in what might be called the English Gypsy tradition. This work is based on years of formal and informal activity related to Gypsy issues. From my earliest days, my family traveled from our East London home to the hop fields of Kent, where I played and worked with a strange and intriguing assortment of Gypsy and Gorgio (non-Gypsy) children. On my sixteenth birthday, I stood on a pub table at Horsmonden horse fair, a regular family event, and sang, to the applause of those I considered to be my people, "I'm a True Didikois." As a teenager, I attended and was repelled by cock- and dogfights. I have witnessed bare-knuckle boxing, both organized and impromptu, at close range. At 3 A.M. on June 17, 1972, in a gravel pit in Essex, I fought one Ryan O'Connell in front of a crowd of Irish Travelers and English Gypsies, losing a purse of £50 an hour later. I have rubbed shoulders with Gypsies and Travelers in the southeastern United States, shared their stories, and read how American theorists have done little more than reiterate European academic perceptions of related groups. I have practiced as a professional youth and community worker with Gypsy families on and off site. I have served on a national organization concerned with Gypsy education and have written, lectured, spoken, and argued about Gypsy issues from Canning Town to the South Atlantic, from Shanghai to Lusaka.

From this position, I offer my book, which is essentially about stories, how they are made, their social force, and what they collectively create. As such, it is about people and what their stories can tell us about the world, stories that through contortion of reality have come to be to called theories about ethnicity and disguised as the truth; but this too informs us about the character of society. I dedicate my effort to make some sense of all this to my mother and father, who have many good stories to tell and thankfully few theories to peddle.

2
The Ethnic Gypsy

Gypsies, as portrayed in the literature concerned with this group, are represented as essentially a consistent, natural, real, eternal, stable, and static phenomena, victims of a host community beyond themselves. The requirement for separateness and authenticity runs through the majority of this material (see Sutherland 1986; Clebert 1963; Okely 1983, 34, 37, 67; and Fraser 1992, 25), wherein Gypsies are taken to be a distinct ethnic group or race. However ethnicity, like race, is used, as a concept, in something of a casual manner in everyday parlance and social analysis, although there is no working, mundane consensus about the meaning of the word. Race, in routine usage, seems to refer to difference in biological makeup, while ethnicity is used to refer to cultural distinction. For all this, the basic definition of ethnicity is tautological: an ethnic group is that which is labeled an ethnic group. But this categorization is useful to academics, politicians, and other social commentators, as they can use it to segment humanity into distinct groups without taking the chance of being accused of racism; deployment of the ethnic label avoids objective, biological categories by introducing subjective distinctions. However, the concept is almost identical to the idea of race; ethnicity might be thought of as race without the biological aspect, but ethnicity, in usage, includes the biological facets of race. In practice, ethnic categories commonly seem to merge racial and cultural explanations of social difference. Ethnic differences in Western society are expressed via values and behavior (cultural norms); so instead of going from the starting point of racial differentiation to the cultural differences inherent in a race, the analysis moves from cultural differentiation to the racial end point. The outcome of both processes is the same: racial differences and ethnic groups retain an essentialist, homogenous identity. This provides a foundation for the idea of multiculturalism, which overestimates the autonomy and homogeneity of ethnic groupings while underestimating the amount of interdependence of cultural forms.

Culture has taken on the role of race; it is understood to be something that one is born into. As a consequence, a cultural history includes the power of biology. Culture represents an exclusivity set in a common past that includes some and excludes others. The past is made teleological and determinist. It has power over the now through notions of roots and tradition.

The expunging of biology from the concept of race, looking through the lens of cultural inheritance, has created a new discourse of race amenable to the post-Nazi period. Cultural debate has reincarnated the assumptions of racial thought, but in a guise that can accommodate the cultural exclusivists and help them to deny their racism.

Given the above, it can be seen that the notions of culture, ethnicity, and race are interchangeable as analytical notions. As such, it is hard to see the catalog of differentiation as anything more than the product of semantic smoke and rhetorical mirrors. This becomes clearer from an ethnographic perspective:

> *My family call themselves Gypsies, but that is just a front—a way of making us special. Really we are just a big 'ol family. People get kept out of college, so they never get to see how it really is. We are no more than the descendants of European workers, like most people in the United States.* (Alphonse, Chicago, 1971)

> *The Old Girl was a proper "Gypo." Her mum and dad were darker than her, even. They looked like Pakistanis. Anyway, the old man wouldn't leave her alone. He would bike down from Canning Town to the site at Bonny Downs every day. She told him to piss off, but he wouldn't take no for an answer. When they got married they moved*

into flats on the Isle of Dogs. He had a fistfight on the cobbles with a great big Irish bloke for that. They got into a house in Churchill Road, Custom House. When that was bombed, mum found Samson Street empty, and we moved in there. (Jim Belton Sr., East London, 1997)

Ivy lived in King Street, Canning Town. She met the feller down hopping, in Yalding. He'd been called up. They got married in Yalding. He owned a caravan. She moved in, and he went to war. When his people moved off, Ivy went with them.

I met our Rose working in Lyon's Corner House. She lived on a local site. We became good friends. That's how she met Harry (my brother). They moved in with my mum in Beartice Street. (Violet, Canning Town, East London, 1997)

I've lived with Rod for nearly three years. He was part of a grunge group. My ma was horrified when we took off in an old bus. I think we paid about forty quid for it. Rod has been traveling since he was a kid, on and off. All we had was a few bits of food and an old mattress. There was about a dozen of us at first, but we were the only ones left last winter. We've only had the trailer for about six months. We bought it off Ted and Joan. I think it's better for Dale (her two-year-old son). *They live on this site. We're respectable Gypsies now* (she laughed). *We're still a bit hippie, though. Rod says we're "Gypie-hippies," but everyone on the site is okay.* (Toni, unofficial site, Chigwell, Essex, 1997)

For the purposes of analysis, I will explore the notion of ethnicity, because in contemporary social discourse it seems to be the most prevalent of the terms used to categorize and separate human beings into discrete types and is the main means of dichotomizing people into Gypsies and non-Gypsies.

Ethnicity: A Genealogical Approach to a Complex Repertoire

Outside of literature focusing on Gypsies, ethnicity is generally understood as a socially constructed phenomenon:

Neither culture nor ethnicity is "something" that people "have" or, indeed, to which they "belong." They are, rather, complex repertoires which people experience, use, learn, and "do" in their daily lives, within which they construct an ongoing sense of themselves and an understanding of their fellows. (Jenkins 1997, 14)

For Foucault:

> The individual is not a pregiven entity which is seized on by the exercise of power. The individual, with his identity and characteristics, is the product of a relation of power exercised over bodies, multiplicities, desires, forces. (Quoted in Gordon 1980, 74)

Ray, whom I came across living in a mobile home on a roadside in Tennessee in 1974, might be seen to exemplify this process:

> We couldn't find rented accommodations, least nothing any good. We had no cash to buy. I've worked every day of my life; we're no white trash, but here we are here. I guess we's Gypsies of a kind (laughs). But it's okay. It's better than living with family!

Alan (cited in Earle et al. 1994, 50–51) also illustrates how social forces impose themselves on identity:

> There are also a lot of negative reasons for traveling. . . . The current housing crisis is a major factor in many peoples' decisions. With the recent rent rises, changes in the law regarding squatters, it is possible that more will be forced onto the road. High rents and constant bills can be traded for a cheap mobile home and few bills. In some cases, the accommodation available is so poor that it does not seem worth paying £50 p.w. in a shared house, which compares unfavourably with a £200 trailer.
> The government's "back to basics" campaign makes housing unavailable to young people, forcing them to live with friends and relatives, . . . or wherever they can.
> Rented accommodation is unavailable to those with limited finances.
> I couldn't pay the mortgage on a flat in Essex.

Foucault confirms this situation theoretically. Subjectivity and the body are at the center of Foucault's thinking and his genealogical method.

> *A form of history which can account for the constitution of knowledges, discourses, domains of objects, etc., without having to make reference to a subject which is either transcendental in relation to the field of events or runs in its empty sameness throughout the course of history.* (1972, 117)

This confirms Solomos and Back's position that

> *ideas about race and ethnicity have been constructed and reconstructed in specific national political environments. . . . This makes it impossible to conceptualise discourses about race and identity as monolithic and unchangeable.* (1996, 99)

For Foucault, the forms of knowledge unusual to our contemporary way of knowing are restricted by what he called "conditions of possibility," or "epistemes," from which they arise and which they reproduce. An episteme is the "total set of relations that unite, at a given period, the discursive practices that produce epistemological figures, sciences, and possibly formalized systems" (Foucault 1972, 191). From this perspective, the body, and the identity it carries, are constructs emerging out of a particular episteme. As such, it is the effect of forces and a problem demanding explanation (Butchart 1998, 14). The group we call Gypsies is thus specific and complementary to the episteme. Gypsy identity is not a consistent, practically unchanging, timeless phenomenon, as most of the literature focusing on this identity suggests.

Wray and Newitz agree with Foucault to the extent that they see identities, in part, as arising out of historically specific social systems. For them, as social groups produce physical objects characteristic in terms of their ideas about ritual, ideology, and interaction, they also create idealized notions of identity that appear to fit a specific way of living. They maintain that

> *it has often been the task of critics and theorists to read such objects and identities as a way of gauging how a particular culture works and why. Recently, cultural critics . . . have suggested new ways to understand human society in the dialectical relationship between material objects and idealized concepts: that is, they each offer a way to use Marx's early*

> *formulation of base and superstructruture as a means to interpret cultural change as it is occurring.* (Wray and Newitz 1997, 6–7)

Wray and Newitz consider the white trash identity as something that can be utilized to consider the nature of identity in contemporary society. Gypsies might be thought of in a similar way. The creation and maintenance of Gypsy identity can tell us something about the society within which that identity is propagated: Gypsy identity can be understood as arising from the dialectical relationship between material objects and idealized concepts and as offering a means to interpret cultural change as it is occurring (1997, 6–7). This process can cause people to join or be conscripted to Gypsy identity. The action of a youth worker practicing within a Gypsy community in the north of England reveals something of this process:

> *We had talked at great length about his views on being a Traveler. He talked about his dark skin and black hair. He saw this as evidence of his Italian origins. To me this is fine. People can claim to come from where they want; but why? This interests me. When I first told him that the Traveling people originally came from India he said, "I'm not Indian!" I went on to explain that this was something like a thousand years ago and that their passage through Europe took a long time, so he might have some Mediterranean blood in him. I also said that he might just have a dark complexion. I lent him a book called* Surviving Peoples, Gypsies. *It was a brief history of Traveling people. It was the first book he had read.*

This young person's perception of himself was redefined through the worker's formed definition of his identity. But why should this young person have more Gypsy blood than anyone else? What is the significance of blood anyway? Was it that he happened to live in a trailer, a flawless defining factor of Gypsy identity?

The Construction of Gypsy Identity

I was raised with the notion that I was different; that others were quite separate from my family. It was never said that "We are

Gypsies," or "They are *Gaje*" (non-Gypsies), but it was understood that we were not like them, and they were not the same as us; we did things that they didn't, and, in truth, we handled this by developing an attitude that we were better than them. There was no straightforward explanation for this conclusion. Who we were served as enough clarification, and what we were was us. But this exclusivity was not a race, nor was it an ethnic type. Those who were not us saw us as, depending on the context of their view of us, among other things, costermongers, robbers, con artists, mumpers, and Gypos. So, it is perhaps not surprising that from a young age I was interested (although truly unconcerned) in the reasons how we were perceived and defined. It seemed certain that how I was seen had something to do with the way my family lived and what we did for work. Our income and how we got it was an aspect of this; but the fact that from the age of five I personally earned money (within the family business activity) and had an extraordinary level of disposable income set me apart. However, this, for me, was simply part of life: the work I did and the money I made were facets of my family life, which itself was connected to a wider set of values presided over and dictated by my paternal grandmother. For all my compliance with and acceptance of these seeming norms, they were, for others, processes and behaviors that they seemed, for the most part, from my perspective, unable to comprehend. My family's waves of income oscillated with the seasons, according to our portfolio of self-employed activity, together with its propensity to acquire the outward trappings of wealth: clothes, jewelry, motor vehicles; and, for my brother and me the latest and most expensive toys that, unbeknownst to our envious childhood peers, were in fact being used by us in transit between being bought and sold. I learned to never love a toy too much, as such things were always in a state of coming and going. Retrospectively, it seems to me that the way my family made a living caused us to be summed up on a continuum that moved from untrustworthy to mysterious and led to responses that started as suspicion and sometimes developed into superstition, fear, and hate; although unseen by them, we had a relatively impoverished existence, living in damp and freezing conditions in the winter, fighting serial bankruptcy, and spending inordinate amounts of time stretching the family food budget with manically judicious shopping habits.

My family way of life and the attitude of the wider community toward us had the effect of turning us in on ourselves. As we were not trusted, so we trusted no one but each other. This caused our way of doing and seeing things to become increasingly ingrained; we became even more us as outside influences grew more remote, aggressive, and, I think foreign, until every encounter with the wider world could be interpreted as a reaction to us, which in the process further confirmed that we were different from them. This was at least a two-sided reaction.

Life was a struggle between us and them; fidelity and loyalty to each other became our credo and what we put our faith in; the godhead was my grandmother. For instance, when I was subjected to bullying at school, it would be inevitable that my family would become involved in setting matters straight. Any oppressor would be held down while I was obliged to give them as good as they had given me; refusal on my part would be met by new threats (toward me) from my family (evoked by my grandmother). This, of course, resulted in my brother and me being subjected to a strange hybrid of respect and resentment that in turn caused a mutual identification and sympathy between ourselves and others who experienced alienation. My brother became a police cadet while I gravitated toward the milieu of 1970s English youth violence and rebellion. I sallied forth in the football wars of the urban wastelands of the last quarter of the twentieth century, while mixing socially with the array of migrant communities that populated the East End of London at that time; my music was black, my clothes were rude boy ominous, mirroring the garments of the young Caribbean buffalo soldiers who fought on arrival; the business life I pursued with my family saw me dancing with Jews, and I became a favored rouge trader of Indian wholesalers. All the time I became more the other, less a product of the norm.

This was my experience as to how the process of being a Gypsy, an ethnicity, worked; it was a kind of machine of perpetual motion that was generated from the outside and, at the same time, was energized from within. My definition of myself interacted with confirmations from the other to define who I was. However, when, in later life, I began to explore the nature of ethnicity, it became clear that the notions of ethnicity and race are quite fragile and vague, and I was confirmed in my view that they are socially generated. But within the literature relating to Gypsies, I found that there is quite a powerful implication that Gypsy ethnicity is not the ineffable phenomenon I had recognized it to be (see Clebert 1963, xvi–xix; Acton 1974, 54; Liegeois 1985, 13; Okely 1994, 34–37, 67; and Fraser 1992, 25, for example). Ideas about blood, heredity, race, and theories of origin or lineage (see Okely 1983, 6–8) couched in aspects of lifestyle (Kenrick and Bakewell 1990, 16, 10, 56–57; and McKay 1996) and self-ascription (Okely 1983, 66) are central in the literature pertaining to Gypsies. At once, Gypsy ethnicity is seen as an inherited state as well as something that can be culturally adopted. The resulting confusion within the collective analysis of this identity is compounded by its lack of consideration for the role of economic, social, intergroup, and interpersonal factors within the development of the ethnic paradigm or narrative of Gypsy identity.

However, a closer look at those with experience of a Gypsy lifestyle suggests that Gypsy identity may not be connected to genetic propensity or blood inheritance. It demonstrates that what might be seen as Gypsy culture can be habituated, modified, abandoned and resuscitated, and related to social and economic situations. This was most powerfully confirmed to me when, at the age of twenty, I crossed the American-Canadian border and made for the greyhound racing tracks of the southern sunshine states. The months I spent making a precarious living by my wits included meetings with representatives of the various itinerant groups and armies of migrant workers that fuel the fires of the American economy, the legions that one weary traveler I met unkindly called "gypsies, tramps, and thieves." (I asked her what one of these she was, and she replied, "Why, none! I'm a rover; a rolling stone. I don't need no name.")

The following is taken from an interview with George, a settled Traveler who gave up caravan dwelling in the late 1970s.

BB: *When did you start traveling?*

G: *We went on the road proper around 1950. During the war I'd been back and forward a couple of times with the evacuation; in between, mum, my brother, and me had lived with my gran. When dad first got back we got a place, but it was in a right state, although it wasn't just that. Dad really couldn't settle. He'd seen a lot in the Far East, and he really wanted to get away from the town. At first we just got involved with summer work, fruit picking and the like, going up to the end of the hop season to the start of the autumn; that meant we could stay in the shelters provided, hopping huts and that. For two or three years we went back to London in the winter, but when dad bought an old van we were moving around full time. By then I'd finished my schooling.*

BB: *How did you live?*

G: *Well, apart from the picking there was plenty of laboring work. We did a bit of totting, too. Scrap got quite big for a while, and I suppose we made a good living. By the sixties me and my brother had brand-new vans, and we had time for the lurchers and a bit of horse trading. We got quite good at that sort of thing, for city boys anyway.*

BB: *Were there any other Travelers in your family?*

G: *No, I don't think so, although my daughter is married to a Gypsy lad. He isn't on the road anymore. They live near Basildon. No, we were the first, as far as I know. I think if we could have had a decent home mum and dad would not have taken up traveling. He would have settled down eventually. But what we had was not all that, and when he first came home, probably because of the work he chose to do, he never got round to saving up enough to put down on a house. By the time he had that kind of cash we had got used to being on the move. He never did settle.*

BB: *Why did you stop traveling?*

G: *It was a case of no longer having to. I was able to do me business from one place. I always saw meself settling down eventually, although my brother still travels in the summer.*

This is one of many interviews I have undertaken over more than a quarter of a century that suggest that there is a consistent link between homelessness and a traveling lifestyle. Adams et al.

(1975, 9) state that a considerable number of nonnomadic people have taken to caravans, while Okely (1983) has seen the British housing shortage lead to a rise in the numbers of people resorting to caravans. But there are all sorts of influences that might incline or dictate that people adopt or find themselves identified as Gypsies.

Billy "Two Hats" lives on the western borders of the English county of Essex and northeast London. Billy's great-uncle was a Welsh Drover. His parents moved into housing in the 1920s, his father having gained permanent employment. He told me:

> Me granddad on me dad's side was down the mines. Grandma came out of service to marry him. Mum was an orphan, brought up on a farm. Dad only started traveling to get out of the mines. He took up with his uncle George. He was a drover, but they did a bit of picking and general farm work, too. When the droving finished, the farm work took over. He carried on moving round for a bit, but then got a cottage on a big farm near Cheltenham. Got involved with looking after the horses and that. He had got a fair bit of know-how from his time droving.

Billy joined the British army in the early 1940s. Following his demobilization in Europe, he purchased a motorbike from a Czech farmer and traveled all over the Continent. After a year, he found himself back in Britain and took up a traveling lifestyle. Billy acquired a surplus Bedford van ("The Crown Hotel") and gradually customized it to facilitate a nomadic existence. Working in the scrap-metal trade all over southeast England, Billy and his brother, former merchant seaman Ron, led a traveling existence for almost ten years. With the demise of the scrap-metal trade the men developed a building supply business. This meant that they gradually had to curb their itinerancy. Ron settled in Sussex where he still lives with his wife, Rene, who comes from a traditional Gypsy family (they met at Paddock Wood horse fair, a traditional event that takes place annually in that town in the English county of Kent). They have a daughter, Clara, who after qualifying as a nurse married a garage owner, Alf. They have two sons, David and Terry. David works for a finance company in

Hong Kong. Terry spent two years in medical school before taking to the road. He lives and travels with his partner Sharla and their three-year-old son Boon. Terry is a veteran road protester.

Billy gave up traveling just before his first marriage but resumed his nomadic ways for a few more years when this relationship ended in the mid-1960s. He is now married to Rene's younger sister, Sal. They settled in Chingford, Essex, in the early 1970s. Billy had one son by his first marriage. He and Sal have two daughters; the elder one, Celia, married into a Gypsy family. She spends part of the year traveling and part running her family fish and chips shop in Brighton, Sussex. Billy and Sal still travel in the summer months. He wants to

> *sell up, buy a big ol' camper and travel across the States . . . or Australia. Traveling ain't in yer blood, it's in yer head. You start out looking to "wipe yer mouth." Now, well, it's just seeing new things, different people. All these old mumpers going on about it "being in 'em." Load of arseholes, that is. You do what you gotta do. You mix with people in the same position, and that's that.*
>
> *When it suited me, I traveled; when it didn't, I stopped. I'll be like that 'til I fall off the twig. Ethnicity? What's that? Most of the ol' Gypo boys I know would have a laugh at that. What you need is a few bob in yer pocket, not a bleedin' ethnicity—that won't buy yer bread and butter!* (laughs)

Ethnic Markers

Much of the literature looking at American Gypsies concerns itself with the markers of Gypsy ethnicity or race (Nemeth 2002; Brown 1924; Sway 1988; Gropper 1975; Sutherland 1986). This search for corporal representation of ethnicity in the everyday activity of groups already defined as Gypsies before the recognition and presentation of these markers mirrors and confirms writers on Gypsy issues in the British European context. The importance attached to these proposed signs as determinants of ethnic affiliation demands that they be analyzed and their relevance examined. In the following I explore and critique some of the main indicators as defined in this literature.

Ritual and Rite

According to Boas (1911), customs, rituals, and habits are of vital importance to the maintenance of societies. He drew on the romantic vision of culture as heritage and habit, the role of which is to allow the past to shape the present. For him, tradition and history mold individual behavior, and culture is generated out of this fusion. For Boas, the particularity of cultures is essential to continued social stability.

For Durkheim (1915), collective representation—the beliefs, values, and symbols that are common to any particular society—serves as a means of perceiving the environment and giving it meaning. According to Durkheim, individual modes of thinking and feeling are shaped by collective representations imposed by the society of which they are a part.

According to Radcliffe Brown, "Every custom and belief . . . plays some determinate part in the social life of the community" (quoted in Kuper 1983, 43). Durkheim goes further than this, arguing that people use ritual to represent to themselves the pattern of relations in society. Durkheim argues that the unit of significance in ritual is the action, as action causes beliefs (not the reverse). So, for him, ritual has a primary epistemological function; the required building blocks of thinking are transmitted through the shared effervescence of ritual. However, Goldschmidt (1990) argues that the use of ritual is most significant "at points of culturally defined crisis which focus on the group and reinforce its unity" (175). According to him, rituals manipulate human feelings to create a common sentiment and reaffirm social ties.

This being the case, rite and ritual, although they are used to mark out ethnic boundaries, appear to be more indicators of general social affiliation. It would seem that ritual and rite are primarily social bonding agents; ritual relates to ethnicity as a secondary effect. Ritual and rite mark out one social or community group, but these cultural markers may not be shared by another group that occupies the same ethnic category. This seems to be the case among Gypsies. However, at the same time, these rituals and rites may be shared with groups outside the ethnic group. For example, Gypsy rites concerning hygiene or cleanliness (Okely 1983, 80–86) can be cynically understood as middle-class and academic interpretations of essentially working-class traditions, homespun lore engendered through a lack of education, inadequate health care, and inherited good advice. My great-aunt Harriet, who came into my family from a settled background, told me of one ritual:

> *My Nan used to have three old bowls. One was always used for washing up, one for washing clothes, and another for any big scrubbing down jobs, like cleaning the backyard. This was because when there wasn't inside taps you'd get your drinking water from one pump and for everything else from another pump that was nearer. So, the clean water was always used for washing up. The water from the wash pump was used for clothes and now and again used for scrubbing jobs and that would stand out in the yard, sometimes for a week, so you had to have a separate bowl for that. Even when she had indoors hot and cold running water she still used the three bowls, but that was as much habit as anything else. But when we told her she could use just one bowl she'd just say, "That's just dirty."*

This illustrates that Gypsy notions of dirt and dirtiness do not significantly differ from those of non-Gypsies, but that ideas of what is clean and unclean are dictated by considerations that may have little to do with clinically related hygiene but are in fact based on behaviors that have habituated out of existing or former pragmatic necessity. The above analysis begs certain questions: Why do we interpret some behaviors as evidencing ethnic membership while regarding other common activity within nonethnic groups, although based on symbolism, rites, or rituals, as having no relationship to ethnicity? Why is the symbolic behavior of football fans or Hell's Angels, which might be seen as ritualistic, not related to a demon angelic ethnicity or a football race? It seems that the use of rites and ritual to mark out ethnicity might be little more than part of a program of self-delusion undertaken by those who have an interest (conscious or unconscious) in the generation of the notion of an ethnic Gypsy type.

Language

Writers on Gypsy issues have consistently seen language as an important marker of ethnic identity, working hard to argue connections with subcontinental traditions. However, in common with ideas relating to ritual and rite, the claims made for language as an effective bonding agent within the homogeneity of the Gypsy population do not stand up to critical scrutiny. Okely (1994, 7), for example, argues:

> *Language moves and changes separately from groups of people. Whether one likes it or not, the prevailing language in Ireland is English. But this does not mean that the Irish are descended from the English! Language gives us clues to some past relationship—for example, colonial conquest or trade.*

Acton (1974, 55–57) makes the case for persistent and widespread use of Gypsy languages to confirm the separateness and distinctiveness of Gypsies. However, language is a brittle marker of ethnicity. Fraser (1992, 22) states:

> *Historical linguistics cannot determine the racial and ethnic origin of early Romani speakers. There is no inherent or necessary link between language and race.*

Even where a whole mode of verbal communication is evident, this does not necessarily indicate a separate language, ancient origins, or a distinct heritage. Donall P. O'Baoill, head of structural linguistics at Institiuid Teangeolaiochta Eireann, has stated that the creation of Irish Traveler Cant came about in the last 350 years. For him, this means of communication doesn't constitute a distinct language, as its structure is indelibly connected to English (1994, 155–69).

This link to a host language is how many Gypsies might understand their use of the so-called Romany as a means of communication set in, related to, and partly arising from wider discourse. Dolly, who was born into an itinerant way of life in 1947, told me,

> *My dad was a navy man. He only took to the road when he came back from the war. By then he'd been at sea for nearly twenty years, and he used a lot of words he picked up, ones that were used at sea and others that he had got when he went ashore in foreign places. He loved words, so he used all that, a bit of rhyming slang and stuff he learnt from other Travelers. I suppose he had a bit of a language of his own in the end. He could chat to those he knew, family and that, and someone else, someone who didn't know us, would think he was using Romany, or something. I can still chat away in it myself, but not as good as him.*

Various activities, and social and employment groups, all have specialized language particular to them. Even alongside unique rituals and rites, dress codes, and social structures, this does not give rise to ethnic categories enveloping such groups.

If one were to look at a housing project in New York and another in Moscow, it is likely that one would find similar traditions and perhaps even shared fragments of language (particularly in respect of consumerist contexts: advertising, television, popular music, and cinema, for example). This does not demonstrate a strong connection between the origins of people. On the contrary, it may be understood as a reflection of the interchange and mobility of cultures. If one goes on to compare the housing projects' rites with those of Gypsies, one could again find similarities, but once again this would not in and of itself demonstrate any linkage, racial or otherwise.

Fraser (1992, 25) relies on connections between elements of language of some communities and the names that a range of nomadic groups give to themselves for his presentation of Gypsy homogeneity:

> *There is, however, at least one ethnic inference to be afforded by the language. It lies in the Gypsies' widespread name for men of their own race.*

Even if one were to accept the debt that the various incarnations of Romany have to languages with their roots in the subcontinent, being the cradle of the Indo-European family of languages, comparative linguistics has suggested that the East is the root source of all European languages, so this has questionable validity as a proof of the Indian origin of the descendants of former users of Romany (Willems 1997, 80).

Languages are not restricted genetically; they are socially learned; they move via political, social, environmental, and geographical channels. It has been suggested that Gypsy groups adapt a core vocabulary to the grammar of the country. They have also been influenced linguistically through trading posts and cultural transmission (Renfrew 1987; Mallory 1989). As such, the move from language to people is not necessarily a logical or an unproblematic step (Willems 1997, 83). For example, a Chinese person living in the United States may speak perfect American English, having command of not a word of Mandarin; but this is no guide to racial identity (Jones 1993, 186–87). On this basis, it is difficult to sustain the place language holds at the center of ethnic identity as a defining element of Gypsyness.

Itinerancy

Mobility is seen by many writers on Gypsy issues to be a marker of ethnic identity; but as Guy (1975, 202) argues, itinerancy as a form of ethnic or racial identification is tenuous. The resort to caravan living may not be one of choice. This was exemplified at a global level when a young Gypsy in conversation with Hillary Rodham Clinton was reported to have stated, "I would like to live in a larger house" (Nando.net 1996, 2). It is also likely that many people living in caravans or involved in an itinerant way of life are not Gypsies (Kornblum 1975, 131). Guy (1975) points out how difficult it is to say anything very certain about Gypsy traits. He critiques Clebert's claim that "the Gypsy is primarily and above all else a nomad" (Clebert 1963, 246), arguing that in countries with the largest numbers of Rom, the majority are sedentary (see Fonseca 1995). Liegeois (1986) argues that not all Gypsies are nomads. According to him, since World War II travel has become difficult, given local authorities, border controls, and in the American context the legal complexity of county, state, and federal policies (see Hancock 1987). The industrialization of the Western world has restricted the economic adaptation of Gypsies, while the accompanying urbanization has made the setting up of camps increasingly problematic. For Liegeois, the strength of Gypsy groups lies not in a shared nomadism but in their diverse lives and their "absorption or borrowing from the cultural environment in which they find themselves." This "is achieved without weakening the essential and distinct collective identity" (Liegeois 1986, 8). Hawes and Perez (1995, 7) also suggest that nomadism is no guide to Gypsyness and that a Gypsy need not be a nomad; and they concede that when discussing the situation of Gypsies it is impossible not to acknowledge

> *that large numbers of people who live in caravans do not conform to generally accepted notions of what is meant by that term.*

According to Sandford, a quarter of those included in the 1967 government survey of Travelers in England and Wales said that they had lived in houses. He also refers to a group of people he became aware of while in the process of research,

> *who, starting as Gorjios, had made the leap into Gypsydom by going on the road, thus forming a new generation of Gypsies.* (1973, 181)

This claim of instant ethnic identity generation is deeply problematic. One might adopt the lifestyle of an Inuit or an indigenous Australian, but this does not mean that one would then be part of a new generation of the group into which one has assimilated. One would not be regarded by society as Eskimo or Aborigine. Can an individual claim identity or even ethnicity or race because they have melted into the host group? This may be possible in terms of entities like nation-states, wherein one may be enveloped within a political or geographical boundary, but the categories of race or ethnicity involve much more inflexible notions that call on concepts relating to internal states of the individual: blood, stock, instinct, and nature. Such facets are reliant on the semimystic genealogy, often supported by selective scientific references to genotypes and inheritance. The adoption of the same by those seen to be Gypsies or wishing for any number of reasons to be understood to be Gypsies, of course, gives credence to the whole pastiche.

The nature of the relationship between itinerancy and Gypsyness appears to be amorphous. There is also uncertainty about what is meant by an itinerant lifestyle: What if one travels within a very restricted area? Is itinerancy necessarily a part-time, full-time, seasonal, or cyclical arrangement? If one lives in a caravan, with and sometimes without the potential to move, is one still a Traveler in a spritual, emotional, or psychological sense? This, together with other considerations presented in this section, demonstrates that the relevance of itinerancy as an ethnic or racial indicator seems minimal.

Self-Identification and Ascription

Self-identification is cited by a number of writers as a means by which a Gypsy ethnicity may be postulated (see, for example, Okely 1983, 72–73). In the context of the United States, Nemeth exemplifies the prevalence and apparent power of ethnic self-ascription relative to Gypsies, writing about what he sees as the appropriateness of spontaneous self-ascription, claiming that "ethnic identity and membership in the American environment are no longer fixed and bounded in time and space, but increasingly flexible and fluid" (2000, 6).

When analyzing the position of Irish Travelers, McCann, O'Siochain, and Ruane argue that

> *It is not a question of historical "fact" to be resolved by historical investigation. The crucial question is how Irish Travelers understand their experience at the present time.* (1994, xiii)

However, self-ascription is perhaps the most problematic marker of Gypsy identity. Just to say, "I am a Gypsy" or that "I understand myself to be a Gypsy" does not imply any consistent or agreed set of criteria. One could mean that one is a wanderer, a mystic, one who lives in a caravan; or it may be that the individual making the claim is a deluded lunatic living in a fantasy world. Statements of this type can mean anything and everything.

However, this very elasticity of self-ascription is appealing to certain individuals who want to belong to a different, exotic, oppressed ethnic group, perhaps feeling that they might gain some kind of kudos, influence, respect, or power from this identity. But this flexibility can have an equally negative impact; one is only who one says one is and no more.

Okely (1975, 60) sees "self-ascription rather than 'objective' traits" as the most appropriate means of identifying Gypsies. This coincides with Barth's view, as cited by Guy (1975, 222). For Barth, an ethnic group is constituted by those who identify themselves as a category that might be distinguished from other categories of the same order. At the same time, this group will be recognized by others. Thus, Gypsy identity is established, for Okely, in terms of commitment to the same (Okely 1975, 60). However, she appears to backtrack on this position, stating that familial and kinship relations are necessary in terms of claiming Gypsy identity (1975, 61). From here, she goes on to make the same kind of assumptions as Miller (1975) and Sutherland (1975, 1986) in the American situation by assuming that various groups of nomadic people are a homogenous ethnic category. This contradictory stance is further complicated by her later claim that Gypsies are connected to and interdependent of wider society (Okely 1983, 35), but that Gypsy status is ascribed by birth, one Gypsy parent being required for a legitimate Gypsy identity (67). She argues that non-Gypsies who marry into Gypsy groups are not to be allowed to forget their origins (68). Okely does not elaborate on how this is achieved, but claims a former Gorgio will be able to participate in day-to-day life and that their children will be incorporated into a given Gypsy community. This interpretation is somewhat confusing when she later states that the biological model for Gypsies is misleading, as many Gypsies are as close to non-Gypsies as they are to Gypsies, although her position is perhaps made a little clearer by her argument that

> *the principle of descent provides a method both for inclusion and exclusion. Thus, Gypsies, like any ethnic group, have procedures for releasing or absorbing a number of individuals without weakening*

their boundaries. Ascription by the individual is subsidiary to the group's continuing self-ascription. (1983, 68)

This position seems to give a secondary importance to descent, it being overridden by group ascription; but it is hard to conceptualize how descent can be subsidiary to ethnic self-ascription. Okely does not show how she established the presence of such a hierarchy. The notion is also problematic, given that identity is not a one-way process, since it needs both social and self-ascription (Jenkins 1996).

Other theorists are no clearer about self-ascription and Gypsy identity. This is exemplified by Rao:

I shall use the word "Gypsy" as a general term to cover all persons claiming to be "Rom," irrespective of their cultural, linguistic, or religious differences; and whatever the degree of their nomadism or sedentarization. (1975, 139)

Having established this position, she follows it with an assertion of "the certitude of a common Indian origin for all the Gypsy groups" (140). The consequence of this standpoint is that if one claims to be a Gypsy one has an Indian origin and identity. This theorization fails to offer substantive evidence or coherent explanation. It seems that the researchers have found no firm basis for theoretically relying on self-identification as a substantive indicator of ethnic identity. In contrast, it appears to be a highly fragile marker of Gypsy ethnicity. The overall impression given by the research in Rehfisch (1975) is that the answer to the question "Who is a Gypsy?" is "A Gypsy is anyone who says they are;" but this is not secure. Another answer to the same question might be someone who has, or says he or she has, one Gypsy parent. Of course, both of these contentions could amount to the same thing. How could anyone reliably check if one's parents were Gypsies? Even if I may be able to prove that my father was a Gypsy and thus justify my own claim to Gypsyhood, in order to substantiate my father's Gypsyness, I would have to show that at least one of his parents was a Gypsy and so on. Given the outsider status traditionally associated with Gypsies, excluded as many of them would have been by choice and circumstance, from the bureaucratic interventions of community and state, it would seem that the reliance on public records would be a tenuous and very limited means by which to establish the Gypsy lineage of all but a very few beyond two generations. For the most part, one would need to rely on hearsay or family legends. Interesting and meaningful as such phenomena are, they cannot be regarded as a concrete foundation on which to build an ethnic identity.

Romanticism

Many writers looking at Gypsy issues romanticize Gypsy culture and lifestyle (for example, Brown 1924; P. J. Lee 2000; W. Lee 1999). O'Nions critically asserts:

> *There is the romanticised image of the Gypsy as a primitive rural character often depicted with a horse and painted wagon.* (1995, 3)

This depiction of a pure yet foreign, rural, roving type, involved in esoteric employment (fortune-telling, for example, or reading palms or a crystal ball) and clan pastimes (bareknuckle boxing, cockfighting) encompasses many of the ethnic markers outlined above, including exotic notions attached to origin, nomadism, tribal affiliations, and language. Concepts of blood and the natural abound. For instance, in Clebert (1963) notions of stock, purity (80), mother tongue, and blood run throughout, but are never really explained. A diverse range of people, "all kinds of real Gypsies, by whatever name they may be known," are seen to "be united in the same love of freedom" and their "eternal flight from the bonds of civilisation, in their vital need to live in accordance with nature's rhythm" (1963, xix). The nobility and grand separateness of the Gypsy, as both victim and free person, dominate the character of this text. Biblical origins are explored alongside what Clebert calls "Gypsy legends." This material is intermixed with historical references to Gypsies that portray them emerging from various exotic locations. He comments on a process wherein almost anyone of an itinerant ilk, looking the least bit foreign, was ascribed as having affinity to Gypsies (1963, 8–25). In the course of this exercise, he notes how Indian scholars show an awkward tendency to name all nomads as Gypsies (1963, 21). Clebert presents a catalogue of historical references to various nomadic peoples and tribes. He defines most of them as Gypsies on the strength that "Gypsies were never given a name except by the natives of the countries" (1963, 27). These are then placed in a chronological and geographical order. The result of collation is presented as the progress of the Gypsy exodus. For Clebert, the clear connection between the basic Gypsy language and the dialects of northern India marks the start of the Gypsy exodus from India that took the form of a sudden scattering of Gypsies over the East (1963, 23).

Clebert represents the extreme of the kind of romanticism found in the literature; but he is called on here to exemplify a trait that many, perhaps most, writers on Gypsy issues exhibit. In his work, he includes all the excesses of this tendency that many academics have since replicated. Indeed, the American literature on Gypsies proliferates and broadens this practice (see Hancock 1987; Gropper 1975; Brown 1924; Sutherland 1975, 1986; and Sway 1988, for example).

The Insipid Pursuit of Ethnic Indication

The above analysis demonstrates that the ethnic indicators deployed in the literature concerned with Gypsies are defective determinants of Gypsy identity. Indeed, the examination of these markers merely confirms that identity in general, and Gypsy identity in particular is, in the main, the product of social considerations rather than primarily a consequence of biology, heritage, or the associated twin offspring of race, ethnicity, and culture. As such, it can be understood that Gypsies are not simply an ethnicity determined partly or wholly by factors related to lineage: Gypsy ethnicity is essentially a product of social considerations.

Conclusion

In this chapter, I have suggested that ethnicity is primarily a social construct. This position stands in opposition to the dominant paradigm found in the literature focusing on Gypsy identity, which argues for the transference of identity by means of blood. This, in effect, proposes a hereditary ethnicity that is not easily distinguishable from a racial categorization. I have also argued that Gypsy ethnicity, founded upon tenuous ethnic and racial markers, is a fragile construct.

In fact and practice, ethnicity is something that is more or less adopted and/or assigned; there are crucial pull and push factors. As a boy my attraction to what some might understand to be Gypsy cultural pursuits or customs was very powerful. While many of my school-age peers were hanging around street corners or played table tennis as the soul vultures did their best to win them for Jesus at the local church youth club, my Gypsy contacts introduced me to stalking pheasant, and they took me into the brutal, fearsome, yet exciting worlds of cursing, dogfighting, and cockfighting. With them, I built my own scrambling motorbikes and raced them; we brewed and consumed various forms of near life-threatening hooch; and I was exposed to a vibrant and fascinating world of gaming, bareback horse riding, poaching, gambling, singing, and moneymaking trading. This interaction took me to bare-knuckle fighting events and once catapulted me to the center of that violent yet adrenaline-intoxicated universe. I found that this dimension was not populated by ethnically pure Gypsies or any particular type of person; each venue was a meeting of worlds; class, culture, and status meant little if anything. One owner of a fighting cockerel was a middle-aged Trinidadian; a Chinese Bethnal Green (another one of London's East End villages) teenage girl owned and trained the most astute poaching lurcher I was to see. For an energetic, restless, imaginative, and intelligent young person, this cosmos of melding offered much more than the norm. Memories of my Gypsy-boy days are a psychic rainbow, a firework show that informs and enriches every aspect and moment of my life. This life encouraged me to read my first books, initially related to horses, dogs, and motorcycles; but then I picked up books on poker, which led me to psychology and biography. I was a Gypsy by blood, culture, and tradition, but the way was paved to literature and a subsequent curiosity about classical music and theater. As I made myself fight with bare and bloodied fists and matched myself on two mad wheels, flying at "a ton" over Bow flyover, I forced myself to listen to vinyl Bach and Beethoven at Canning Town library until my mind became attuned and addicted. I used the money I accrued to buy concert and theatre tickets. I saw few lone working-class boys at the Royal Festival Hall or the National Theatre, but I made new friends—Arthur Miller, Harold Pinter, Steven Berkoff, Tchaikovsky, and Vivaldi—who seemed to understand my condition, my frantic feelings; the caravans of my Gypsy mind were moving—I was traveling! An alternative route might have been the respectable yet impoverished apprenticeship, an early marriage, the hell of being locked into a domestic incarceration and the chains of a mortgage, tethering me to a few square yards of sterile earth for a third of a century of toil, untidy affairs, anxiety, care, illness, stress, a pension, divorce, and clinical depression. But all that never happened. Instead—I traveled. *That's why I'm a true Didikois.*

3

Defining American Gypsies

The Inside Outsider

I look at the American Gypsy horizon as an outsider; as someone from Britain I am an outsider commentating as an outsider. This has its drawbacks. Although I have gathered some insight into the experience of American Gypsies, I am not exactly a participant observer. For all this, my background disallows me to be wholly characterized as another interested academic; as such, I am an inside outsider. Such a perspective offers an objectivity that, in the confused and contradictory environment of American Gypsy studies, may provide some much-needed clarity. To grasp the need for this clarity, it is necessary to review what has become the tradition of deciphering Gypsies in the United States.

American Gypsy Studies

The writing focusing on American Gypsies identifies a number of forces that are used to postulate a supposed connectivity between Gypsy populations and their difference from other groups. The deployment of this handful of signifiers to separate and coagulate Gypsies mirrors a similar process within the wider literature

(British and European) relating to Gypsies, which seeks to establish grounds for or factors of distinctions between Gypsies and non-Gypsies. However, the perceived nature of difference in the writing relating to Gypsies is, overall, characterized by reference to behavioral and psychological factors that overlay a more covert notion of the biological Gypsy: a Gypsy race or ethnicity. At the same time, the consideration of the role of broader social issues on the development of what is seen as the Gypsy population is conspicuous by its absence. This position in effect determines Gypsy ethnicity as a behavioral or psychic phenomenon that is passed on via heritage and inheritance. It is not the purpose of this book to find a reason for this, but it was the exclusion in the literature appertaining to American Gypsies of any substantial analysis of the part that social considerations play in defining Gypsy ethnicity—which amounts to a practical rejection of the widely accepted notion that ethnicity is a social product—that provoked a critical reading of material relating to American Gypsies and enabled the development of the focus that this book develops on some of the social processes impacting the generation of Gypsy populations.

It is not possible to embark on any analysis relating to Gypsies without grasping the nature of the notions and theory that surround this group. The literature relating to Gypsies is complex in its diversity and quality. It ranges from stories, biographies, or collections of anecdotes (Sampson 1997; Fonseca 1995; Stewart 1997; Brown 1924) to disciplined and rigorous academic studies (Okely 1983; Sutherland 1986; Gropper 1975; Sway 1988; Acton 1974) and the beginnings of a sociohistorical approach (Willems 1997; Lucassen, Willems, and Cottaar 1998). All of this material has at least some interpretative value in terms of understanding the position and perception of Gypsies. I will use the term "Gypsy," because this seems to be the most widespread term in the American context, and also because the distinction between Gypsies and what might be seen as other or related groups (Rom, Travelers, etcetera) is problematic, there being no agreement about the boundary between these labels (see, for example, Hawes and Perez 1995, 7) and some doubt concerning the integrity and authenticity of the same (Willems 1997, 17–34).

The field of literature called on in this chapter (and throughout the book) represents the most influential thinking referring to the historical, sociological, cultural, and anthropological analysis of Gypsies in the contemporary period. It relates to the topics of central concern to this book: identity and how it is socially generated. What might be called the discipline of Gypsy studies has developed through a number of phases. Willems (1997) has shown how those who might be seen as the founders of this pursuit—Grellmann, Borrow, and Ritter—followed a path pocked with the flaws inherent in romanticism, fantasy, exaggeration, prejudice, and discrimination, premised on hearsay, myth, and the dated vestiges of propaganda, with roots in various premodern European states. Clebert (1963) was one of the first to bring the spirit of this literature into modern discourse, albeit spasmodically veneered with watery sociological and anthropological terminology. Although subscribing to the critique of Clebert's position, which grew in the last decades of the twentieth century, Acton (1974), perhaps unavoidably, almost certainly not purposefully or consciously, replicated many of the flaws of his predecessors in the field of Gypsy studies. This laid the foundation of the Gypsy studies paradigm, in the British and European context, which has been developed and largely dominated by the likes of Okely (1983), Fraser (1992), Liegeois (1985, 1986, 1994), Kenrick and Clark (1995), and Hawes and Perez (1995). While the sociological and anthropological rigor of this material varies across and within any particular example of the genre, in the main, the underlying influences are not too far from those that motivated and energized Borrow and Grellmann. While Willems (1997), Lucassen, Willems, and Cottaar (1998) (collectively known to the field as the Dutch School), and Mayall (1988 and 1995) have done much to challenge this dominant discourse relating to Gypsy studies, analysis of the literature relating to American Gypsies (see, for example, Nemeth 2002; Hancock 1987; Sway 1988; Gropper 1975; Lockwood and Salo 1994; Sutherland 1986; Brown 1924) indicates that it has followed and replicated the prevailing British and European position. From the earliest days of the study of Gypsies in the American context, this mirroring of analysis has been evident. For example, Brown

(1924) has been called "the American Borrow" (Nemeth 2002, 207). In the mid-1970s, Sutherland and Gropper produced the same kind of in-depth research activity in the American context as that which Okely, Rehfisch, and Acton had pursued a few years earlier in the British situation. Sutherland concentrated on the social structure of Gypsy communities while Gropper focused on developing a notion of a system of Gypsy cultural expression. By the mid-1990s, Lockwood and Salo (1994) had produced an exhaustive annotated bibliography of material relating to the various incarnations of Gypsy life in America. As Lockwood and Salo concede, the book provides a "descriptive rather than evaluative" (1994, 12) resource, concerning itself with the formulations of distinctions between Gypsy groups, how representatives from those thus identified see themselves, and the reaction of non-Gypsies to Gypsies. Lockwood and Salo saw the body of social and anthropological interpretations of American Gypsies as clarifying "the concepts of ethnicity among North American Gypsy groups" and concluded that this illustrated the need for each group to be studied on its own and that, by regarding each culture as a system, the study of Gypsies had been liberated from the "obsession with seeking explanations for elements of culture in distant origins." According to Lockwood and Salo, this has enabled the establishment of "the validity of Gypsy cultures in their present contexts" (1994, 6–7). This, of course, makes no sense in terms of the practice of anthropology. As Geana (1997, 65) argues, a disciplined scientific inquiry in this field must be judged by its capacity to understand, as a complete entity, the object it is focused on. This being the case, the explanation of a Gypsy whole made up of hardly numerable discrete cultures is nonsense.

Hard on the heels of Lockwood and Salo, Tong (1995) produced another annotated bibliography that encompassed a huge range of material as diverse as photography and anthropology, psychology, and folklore. This book is a confusing attempt at evaluation, which by Tong's effort to demonstrate "non-Gypsy denial or devaluation of the Gypsies' humanity" generates a Gypsy identity out of an accusatory flux, charged with allegations of racism and an almost evangelical firebrand evocation of collective social guilt, and as such Tong replicates many of the conclusions reached by her contemporaries in the British context (Hawes and Perez 1995).

The impression given by much of the literature is that those groups loosely labeled as Gypsies are a homogenous ethnic group and/or race (or maybe a racial grouping made up of a number of ethnicites: see Hancock 1987, for example). Although there are various categories of Gypsy types within the panorama of the American Gypsy population, they are identified as, and referred to under, the collective label of "Gypsy" and portrayed within a continuity of history and origin. However, my research has indicated that traveling or itinerant ways of life are constructed from a diversity of social, psychological, spiritual, familial, and economic considerations and that these pathways to Gypsyhood seem to not only generate particular types of Gypsies but also bring the whole notion of a homogenous Gypsy population into question, this grouping being made up of, in reality, a diverse range of people with vastly different backgrounds, origins, and perceptions of themselves. Interviews with Gypsies elicit responses like:

> *My granddad was a farmer, but my grandmother was a Gypsy.*

> *There are no Gypsies, just folk who call themselves Gypsies, because it suits them or they think it's what folk want to hear. . . . I can and do call myself a Gypsy when it suits me, . . . but I don't think I'm a Gypsy.*

> *I'm a Gypsy . . . Gypsy born and bred. . . . My mom was a full-blood Cherokee, and my dad was a Polish Jew. . . . He came to the U.S. after World War II, . . . but I'm a Gypsy all right.*

Other sources confirm this complexity:

> *One of my earliest memories was when I myself was about three and a half years old. My brothers Paddy and James and myself were living with my grandfather and mother in their house.* (Bridget Gaffey) (Southwark Traveller Women's Group 1992, 35)

> *I lived in a house and was born in a house.* (Helen Gaffey) (1992, 69)

> *I remember when I was a year old. . . . I was at my granny's house.* (Joannie McDonagh) (1992, 73)

Many people I have asked about how they became involved in a Gypsy lifestyle relate to a tradition or culture (although these particular words are hardly ever used by respondents), portraying the beginnings of their way of being to be lost in time:

> I was born a Gypsy. Me father was a Gypsy, as was his father. Both were born on the wagon.

This initial story of lineage is often modified after I become more familiar with a person and his or her family and other families known to him or her:

> Me father was on the buildings in Dublin. When I was a boy we moved up to Belfast for the work, but what with the family being Catholic and coming from the south, it was hard to get a house. Me uncles had put themselves in trailers, and the trailer was better than what housing there was. Me brother got some work in England on the roads. The firm he was with put him in a trailer by the site. As they made the road, so they moved along with it. He got me in on this, and I was going backward and forward between here and there as the work turned up. But after a while it was easier to stay in England, what with the kids and all. So I do bits and pieces between any work I could get. But the work got less and less until now there's no casual stuff at all. I've gone back to Ireland, but things are worse there.

This story illustrates one of the many routes of Gypsy life. The search for work, housing provision, and sectarianism all seem to have played a part in defining this person and his family. There are, of course, a plethora of other motivations:

> Originally I come from New York. My dad was a sailor as was my grandfather. My mom done what work she could. Her dad had been a furniture maker. I met my wife, and we were married within a month. We started traveling nearly straight away, and did so for about twenty years. Up to two years ago, we did a bit of everything.

This personal story, what might be thought of as a Gypsy way of life, is typical of many of the recollections I have come across. It can be seen as indicative of the historical overlapping between cultures and diverse groups that make up the population thought of as American Gypsies. Such stories have similarities with others all over the world:

> A house dweller may start a relationship with a Traveler and join that partner. (Earle et al. 1994, 50)

> My earliest memory was when we were living in a very old house beside the cathedral. . . . In Ireland I always lived in a house. So when I got married I had to move into a trailer. (Mary Theresa McDonagh) (DTEDG 1992, 55)

> My father was born in Athlone, and my mother was born in Kilkenny. My father lived in a house in Athlone. My mother told me they used to travel all over Ireland, and that was how she met my father. He would come to the camp on a bike to chat with mammy. (Margaret McDonagh) (Dublin Travellers Education and Development Group 1992, 62)

It is impossible to say how many people have moved in and out of any Gypsy population by way of marriage or by adoption of the lifestyle by some other route. It is equally unfeasible to guess if there has been a net contraction or growth in the Gypsy population by way of cultural migration. Okely (1975) found that over 26 percent of couples living together with whom she had close contact included at least one non-Gypsy. More than a quarter of these couples had no Gypsy background at all. What seems certain is that throughout the modern era there has been a sustained and appreciable intermingling between the settled population and Gypsies.

From the above, it is clear that any Gypsy grouping is likely to be the product of cultural and biographical differences and diverse social influences. It would seem that the personal histories of Gypsies move across distinct cultural and social borders and categories, and as such the population cannot be said to be an ethnic whole in any feasible way.

Lucassen et al. (1998) support this perspective while critiquing Fraser (1992), one of the seminal writers supporting the predominant paradigm of Gypsy identity that presents this group as a strange ethnic or racial group consisting of heterogeneous elements yet constituting a homogeneous whole:

> The possibility that through a process of labeling other itinerant groups have become known as Gypsies as well and in the end have

> *internalized this image, or the fact that many Gypsies intermingled with others from the end of the Middle Ages onwards, make only minor inroads in his ideas. Moreover, he too easily discards the possibility that the "people" concept is a fairly recent phenomenon, triggered by nineteenth-century nationalistic ideology and not in the least promoted by the Gypsy Lore Society itself, in which footsteps he clearly follows.* (Lucassen et al. 1998, 6; see appendix for details of the Gypsy Lore Society.)

Recent publications concerned with American Gypsies have suggested that this field

> *lacks credibility, reinforces dangerous stereotypes, tends to mislead, and . . . is redundant in error rather than self-correcting.* (Nemeth 2002, 239)

At the same time,

> *the empirical foundations for scientific Gypsy studies remain incredibly weak.* (Nemeth 2002, 239)

For all this, situated under many titles (for example, Rom, Romanichels, and Romany) and even more numerous subcategories (Russ, Kalderasa, and Meksikaja, for instance), the ethnic or racial Gypsy is today part of the American identity prospect. Most of the literature concerned with the derivation of this population (for example, Gropper 1975; Lockwood and Salo 1994; Hancock 1987; Sway 1988; Brown 1924; Nemeth 2002) depicts Gypsies as having a more or less unproblematic and distinct genesis within the social milieu that is the United States. This lineage is set within a heritage of enforced movement and persecution, embodied in Hancock's (1987) social psychological notion of a pariah status and tends not to give appropriate consideration to social conditions, context, activity, and interaction that may contribute to the development and maintenance of this population. It is my purpose in this book to offer an analysis of this seemingly accepted etiology or prevailing paradigm of the origins of American Gypsies that will provide an American backdrop to the broader examination of the narrative of Gypsy ethnicity. I hope, in turn, it offers the opportunity for some reflection on the part social forces play in the generation of the notion of a Gypsy population, race, or ethnicity through a more sociological perspective on the development of this group, and in particular the role of narrative in this process.

As Nemeth (2002, 239) illustrates, American Gypsy studies can at least be understood as an undisciplined social science, and it contains much the same flaws as the British and European tradition in this field. Hence, the critique of the former that is included in this book can be understood as an attack on the progenitor and motivator of the American incarnation of Gypsy studies (see Nemeth, 235–36), but the latter is implicated in this examination by association.

Defining American Gypsies or any ethnic cultural groups starts with the task of determining who does the defining. The categorization of a group of people by a bigot, an academic, or even a recognized or legitimate Gypsy who says "they, those people there, are/are not Gypsies," albeit this identification is premised on evidence, is unsatisfactory, especially if those thus labeled do not see themselves as such. Certainly, the first book I ever picked up that referred to Gypsies (Clebert 1963) rang few bells for me in terms of my experience. Acton (1974) seemed no less remote from my actuality (although a little less comical). As I roamed around the United States as a young man in my twenties, I looked for the same kind of release with regard to Gypsy studies as I had found in American literature and art; I wanted a theorist who would unshackle this aspect of my consciousness in the way Ernest Hemingway and Edward Hopper had opened other vistas. Unfortunately what I found—comparing it to my experience of encounters with "real" people, those who were called or called themselves American Gypsies— seemed little more than recontextualized versions of the disappointingly myopic texts I had frustratedly waded through in Britain. At that time, I did not know what to do with my growing angst, which became worse as my curiosity merely confirmed my irritation with my reading. At the same time, I got to be known, within the tight social milieu in which I was making a living, as "the Limey looking for Gypsies." As I traveled, I was also devouring everything I could find from the pen of

Bruno Bettelheim, and it was this part of my peripatetic studies, which elaborated the concentration-camp experience and linked it to the autistic phenomenon, that first alerted me to the danger of the categorization theorized and prescribed first in European and then in American Gypsy studies. I felt a kind of slow-motion but developing panic deep within me. I had to do something, but all I did for a while was talk to people. Then I began to keep a scruffy diary of these conversations and my impressions of them. It wasn't until I met Kathy, a waffle-house waitress whose grandparents, she informed me, had come to America as Irish Tinkers, that I gained some definition of the questions I wanted to ask. It was a question from her to me, rather than the other way round, that summed up my complex feelings at that time:

> *Even if a man agrees to be called a Gypsy, the question still nags away in the background: "Who started this naming, and why?"*

Snowbirds and Gypsies

Kathy's question (as I referred to the above quandary for some time) seemed to be at least partly addressed via a social trend in the United States. For more than three decades, each season an increasing number of mostly older people from all over the United States have loaded up their RVs, Winnebagos, and other mobile homes and driven south to Florida to spend three or four months taking advantage of the weather. Because of their migratory behavior, this population has come to be known as "snowbirds." However, a significant number of these migrants have adopted a near itinerant way of life, choosing to live a mobile or semimobile existence on a temporary, long-term, or permanent basis.

This group has developed alongside Florida's traditional winter visitors, which includes homeless people looking to escape the harshness of the northern winter (arriving approximately as the first snow falls in the northern states) and groups of traditional Gypsies that may or may not have a relationship with the relatively large settled Gypsy population in Miami and wider Florida.

I met David, a forty-eight-year-old homeless man from Detroit, at the West Flagler dog racing track in Miami. He was spending the winter in Orlando. He told me,

> A lot of people come here looking to get work. A few want to start over, but it is an easy place just to live on the street. I get here earlier than most, around the end of September. This year I worked in New York for a spell and got the money for a one-way Greyhound ticket down here. I can't take the weather up north no more.
>
> I got a daughter and a ten-year-old granddaughter back in Detroit, and I'll go back there around April or when it gets too hot here. Before this year I'd winter in one of the homeless shelters, but every year they are harder to come by, as so many people come down here now. I think a lot of them are Gypsies. I met up with a guy who recently lost his wife. He lives down here permanent in his Winnebago, so I'm going to pay him for a bed and stuff. I guess I'll get some work in construction; I've done that before. You just turn up at daybreak with everyone else and pick up a job. But I need to get some workboots first. So first off I'll get some money picking, but it's going to be harder this year. A lot of them Gypsies from Europe grab the work. They work in groups you see, sometimes going from house to house.
>
> Trouble is now no one knows who is a Gypsy and who is not! Lots of them arrive in trailers, and they could be taken as just people who come down for the winter like everyone else. In the same way, I can get taken to be a Gypsy. Because I didn't have no boots the guy says, "You're a Gypsy!" I says, "I'm not no Gypsy. I'm from Michigan." But they take no notice. It's stupid anyway. Half those guys they are calling Gypsies are as American as me, born in the USA. Some just spend the summer working for some uncle or something. But for some it suits to just let it be. Any way you can, I guess. It's all about getting a place to live and some work.

The disinterested and largely unconcerned spectator might take the immediate and surface appearance of David's existence to be or look like the life of a Gypsy. But this complex and intriguing life path was one of many I came across that might superficially fit such a convenient stereotype. However, David's story exemplifies any number of reasons why someone or some group can call itself or become known as Gypsies. At the same time, it does not seem unreasonable to speculate that those whom we call or recognize as Gypsies do in fact come from a range of cultural and ethnic backgrounds. Lucassen et al. (1998) go much further than others in demonstrating that Gypsies derive from various origins (see especially Cottar in Lucassen et al. 1998, 114–52) and critique what they call "the inadequacy of traditional answers" (1998, 1–16) found in research surrounding Gypsies and other itinerant groups. But even they continue a traditional, if uneasy, consensus within the literature that recognizes a population, which might be thought of as a single entity, made up of a diversity of ethnic types, where inclusion into the whole seems to be based on rather open qualifications. Academic activity and writing on Gypsies generally have ignored the phenomena—replicated worldwide—that are encompassed and fueled by people like David.

Self-Ascription

It might be reasonable to ask if snowbirds could be considered Gypsies. Of course, the most obvious Gypsy trait to the outside world is itinerancy, so it would seem the most likely persons to be Gypsies would be ones who ascribe this label to themselves and who habitually travel (are not sedentary for most of the time) as a way of life. But this seems a vulnerable and uncertain measure of ethnicity and not applicable to many who might call themselves Gypsies in America and Europe. For many writers, calling oneself a Gypsy seems to be a major factor in terms of establishing Gypsy identity (for example, Okely 1983, 68–69).

This situation is further complicated in the American context by the presence of the kind of analysis exemplified by Nemeth, who recognizes a "spontaneous self-ascription . . . ethnic identity and membership being no longer fixed and bounded in time and space, but increasingly flexible and fluid" (2002, 6). Astonishingly enough, Nemeth goes on to soundly critique his own conclusions by admitting that his approach is a "pastiche of intellectual and emotional scholarship, and not strictly scientific" (2002). One finds it hard to argue with this latter point. Self-ascription seems to have more in common with the Popeye postmodern church of identity than anything rational: "I yam what a yam, and that's all that I yam (for now, anyway)."

However, Rehfisch (1975) and Nemeth (2002) are among the few writers concerned with Gypsy identity who overtly state that the main marker of Gypsy identity is self-ascription; and it seems that the social categorization of Gypsy is, at least in part, created by groups and individuals in the wider social field that include academics of the type who write about Gypsies (see Willems 1997; 1998, 29–32). Given the feelings of ethnic discontinuity that appear to exist within the Gypsy community (see Okely 1983, 72–73), those groups comprising the category Gypsy would seem less likely to see themselves as part of a tight whole than interested non-Gypsies.

One People

This is perhaps unsurprising in that Gypsies are not one people, just as Asians are not one people. I often balk when I hear professionals claim they are working with or in the Chinese community. When I was working in China, I attended a seminar at the University of Hong Kong conducted by a specialist in Chinese languages who told of there being around fifty million languages and dialects spoken in China, which of course is a vast place, full of very different people. As such, one might reasonably ask, "What is the Chinese community? How might we find anything more than some superficial commonality?" In the same way, one may question the notion of an Asian community. Is this entity, so often referred to in professional and media parlance, referring to Indians, Pakistanis, Sri Lankans, Bangladeshis, South Koreans, Australians, or all of these groups and all the groups that make up these groups? However, it is perhaps more likely that when someone talks about the Asian community they are alluding to local brown people, and, this being the case, the moniker smacks of a kind of racism; the practice of lumping people together in this arbitrary fashion is a violent and seemingly thoughtless act, be the people Asian, Chinese, or Gypsy. As someone with a number of connections with the latter group, I do not somehow represent a whole, and I have never met a

Gypsy, apart from those with a vested political or financial interest, who believed he or she does either.

Limited Anthropology

The literature focusing on Gypsy identity relies heavily on forms of a limited anthropological analysis. For example, Lucassen et al. assess Fraser (1992) as representing the tradition of Gypsy research. As they state, Fraser displays a vast knowledge of the existing literature. But, Lucassen et al. argue, his analysis is mainly leaning on linguistic research and upholding

> *the view that Gypsies have to be considered a people with Indian roots, who would have succeeded in keeping their ethnicity intact since they fled their country of origin.* (1998, 5)

For Lucassen et al.,

> *this interpretation is not unproblematic and is in many respects based on speculation mixed with a fair proportion of teleological and wishful thinking. Fraser and others with him refuses to integrate competing evidence in his analysis and only uses what fits with his preconceived idea of one Gypsy people.* (1998, 6)

The type of analysis used by Fraser has influenced most of the ideas relating to Gypsy identity, and the rigor of the total enterprise has varied greatly. Most of the research has been guilty of flagrantly overemphasizing the role of genealogy and/or heritage in establishing Gypsy identity, to the extent that one is left with an analysis that is overwhelmingly propagating an ideology of biological determinism. This has been covertly or overtly postulated in the form of a Gypsy ethnicity or related concepts such as race and culture. For example:

> *Roma, commonly known as Gypsies, are a traditionally nomadic people found throughout the world. The Roma share a common biological, cultural, and linguistic heritage that sets them apart as a genuine ethnic group.* (Encarta Online 1998, 1)

To a large extent, this position ignores the sociological and everyday (macro) social context within which the very diverse groups that make up the Gypsy population exist (Willems 1997, 17).

The Contorted Gypsy

In short, the position that arises out of limited anthropology—the notion of one Gypsy people joined by the diversity of its parts and the seeming magic of self-ascription—is that "Gypsies are there because they are there and because people say they are" and is acceptable because "Gypsies defy commensuration," which is "the turning of things into numbers," and "this 'thing' called the Gypsy . . . cannot be counted and mapped" (Nemeth 2002, 4). This type of twisting and turning of reality (which is typical of the literature appertaining to Gypsies) works to confirm and perpetuate the mystic tradition surrounding the Gypsies. Those groups thus labeled become a kind of jabberwocky of ethnicity, corralled as a mythical tribal people, a cryptic group, which, as such, is vulnerable to the Humpty Dumpty school of social anthropology, whose adherents, looking to develop their own profile as esoterics, cobble identity together out of anecdote, pastiche, or romantic parody, making phenomena mean just what they want them to mean, neither more nor less. It is tempting to assert that no sane or coherent social analyst could reasonably accept this as unproblematic. However, it may be enough to suggest that the erection of such fragile ethnic structures might prove to be at least irresponsible and maybe even dangerous. The creation of difference on the strength of whim, ephemeral sign, or trace evidence, or merely "the way I feel" may have unseen repercussions or unforeseen consequences (see Montagu 1997).

Diverse Origins

I met Henry at the Southland greyhound track in West Memphis. He told me,

> When I was fifteen, I said to my mom that one day I would sail around the world. And she said to me, "You can do whatever you like,

Henry. Your dreams are as near as your heart will let you come." But I was forty-eight when I finally gave everything up to live my dream. By the time I got back I was fifty-eight. I tried to settle down, but I couldn't get used to it. So when I met Sophie it was not hard to take up a traveling way of life. I'm seventy-three now, and we've been together and traveling for close to thirteen years. I have two sons, both born on the road. Sophie has always traveled around with her family. We make our way 'round. There's Sophie's brothers and their families and some cousins. We are not all together all the time. But we all meet up at Thanksgiving and Christmas, and everyone is always in touch. But her dad was a carpenter in Albania before he came to the United States. He traveled around getting work where he could. I guess he just went on moving.*

Henry is one of a group of people habituated to traveling the world by sea as boat owners or unpaid crew. In any number of ports around the world they are becoming known as sea Gypsies. I met Gary, the owner of the sixty-foot *Sea Horse*, in Stanley harbor in the Falkland Islands. Gary was fifty-four and had been at sea for nearly twenty years.

I must have been around the world a couple of times. I was born in Louisville, Kentucky, but I did my medical training in Scotland. I never finished. I took up traveling in the summer of 1971, all over Britain and France, down to Spain and Portugal. We were just hippies or crusties I suppose. It was in Lisbon that I met this woman, and she was looking for a crew to sail back to the States. I knew nothing about sailing and just learnt as I went along, between throwing up. There were four of us. When the voyage was over she gave us the boat as a sort of payment and it went on from there. People came and went. Some pay, some just work passage, and I've just traded craft as I've gone along. I gave my old boat and $1,100 for this (the Sea Horse*). It needed a lot of work, but it's fine now. I think the sea is the final frontier on earth. That's the attraction of the life. But I think I'm also a born rover. It's just in me. A lot of people are doing what I do, many couples, families. There are also people who started out with wives, husbands, girl- or boyfriends; but living in cramped, hard conditions is quite a test for any relationship.*

Stanley has become something of my base camp. It is here I check my e-mail and buy supplies. But it's great to find some lonely an-

chorage, some lovely bay with dolphins swimming around your boat, or you can stroll on a beautiful beach alone.

Some people spend more time anchored in one spot, taking time to form relationships with local people. Some have contacts on islands all over the world. I have had to work to get money at times. I've done a bit of everything: electrician, laborer, plumber, even a canvas maker. It takes quite a bit of money to keep this life going. Maybe $10,000 a year. It is, for most people, a life of poverty, and, yes, there are times that I literally have to fish for my supper. I don't know how much longer I can keep the life up. It does get harder every year. But I'll always travel. I suppose when I have to give this up I'll just go back to what I did before I started. Maybe I'll become a real Gypsy!

Like other narratives included in this book, Gary's story of intent and activity demonstrates the potential for the expansion of the definition of what constitutes a Gypsy and the diversity of the existing Gypsy population. Collectively this calls into question ideas relating to Indian or other specific derivations and seems to contradict the research concentrating on American Gypsies—for example that of Sway (1988) and Sutherland (1986)—that perpetuates the mystification of the nature of the Gypsy population, portraying Gypsies as the same but different, connected but separate, and that obviates the need for a multidisciplinary exploration of the American Gypsy population.

Sameness Equals Difference: An Ignoble Equation

That the literature concentrating on Gypsies recognizes the multifarious character of this population, but at the same time contains an undercurrent that seems to argue for Gypsy connectivity, often premised on vague racial or ethnic foundations, is problematic. It suggests a tenuous collective of Gypsyness, grouping people together around fragmented similarities of language, ritual, or tradition, while for the most part demonstrating little correlation between these considerations. For example, a group may share snippets of language, but have very different lifestyles. The overall exercise would not be dissimilar to an attempt to define contemporary Americanness or Irishness, for example, in terms of habit, tradition, or even language.

The effort to present the idea of a homogenous Gypsy population, implying that this grouping constitutes a whole race made up of a number of different ethnicities, creates an obvious tension that is premised on an insistence on an underlying or primal unity that is built on the basis of diversity. For example, Acton at points argues against a clear or distinctive racial or ethnic Gypsyness, seeing the Traveler population as a "disunited and ill-defined people," who possess "continuity, rather than a community, of culture" (1974, 54). However, he makes many statements that suggest distinctive origins and ethnic categories, for example, referring to Romany speakers leaving India one thousand years ago (1). He suggests the presence of a caste hierarchy (54), but goes on to question the validity of this, arguing that one sociocultural continuum (58)—or a number of them—exists in relation to Gypsies. Acton's position is further complicated by his definition of different categories of Gypsies (60–78) and the responses of some of those he categorizes:

> *My great-uncle came from drover stock in Wales. They'd drive anything. Cattle, geese, turkeys—anything with legs. The trade didn't die overnight, though. There was still some short-range work before the first war. But they had to take other things up. Any kind of farm laboring, roundups, even tinkering. Gradually that's all there was, and a lot of folk turned it in. But I reckon most of those traveling in Wales have drover blood. I've heard the idea that we come from India or that some Gypsy people do, but that makes no sense. Most people I've ever come across have come from all sorts of places, and I've never heard a one say they's from India. All that is a bit of a joke.*

Acton is arguing that Gypsies are a distinct group but presents diversity as a key factor (54). Social and cultural identity are not central to Acton's theoretical analysis; his primary concern seems to be to present a homogeneity of difference.

Hancock (1987) broadly follows Acton's position in the American context, and, although he argues that Gypsy identity is seen as problematic, the idea of a definite racial or ethnic group is energetically propagated.

Liegeois takes more of a worldwide view of the history and character of Gypsies. He consistently makes the point that what he is looking at when referring to Gypsies is "a rich mosaic of ethnic fragments" (1986, 13), a collection of different groups with different names. He can thus be understood to agree with Acton's interpretation. He argues for an overall connection between these groups, although this is fragile and tenuous in nature. Liegeois argues that the world population of Gypsies is the sum of small diverse groups (1986, 49). For him, Gypsies are connected by a flexible and constantly changing structure, which is derived from their consistent persecution.

For all this Liegeois seems to challenge his own position, contending that contemporary studies of Gypsies are inaccurate, because they do not allow for the very complex and multifaceted reality (1986, 49) of Gypsy identity. He describes portrayals of Gypsies as slanted by overgeneralization and based on stereotypical images, which are hundreds of years old. He argues that such a group cannot be adequately described in generalities, any synthesis (1986, 49) necessarily being an oversimplification. At this point, Liegeois seems to hold a dual understanding: Gypsies can be taken to be a very diverse, loosely connected group, but at the same time we must see this synthesis as doubtful.

According to Liegeois (1986), Gypsy culture is not unchanging or passive. The diverse grouping that he refers to as Gypsies cannot really be thought of as having a straightforward line of development. Although he does use generalization throughout, he constantly reiterates that the character of those groups that share Gypsy identity is diverse. Reinforcing this point, he informs his reader that there is no single word for a Gypsy type in the various Romany dialects. This contradicts the likes of Clebert (1963), Fraser (1992), and Hawes and Perez (1995), but it is a much more secure analysis in the light of Willems (1997) and Lucassen et al. (1998); Willems shows the basic historical analysis of Gypsy origins to be spurious, while Lucassen et al. clearly indicate that the ethnic label "Gypsy" is primarily socially generated.

Much effort is expended in the literature justifying the exotic version of Gypsy origins, tradition and language being cited as cementing factors. This argument, as Liegeois (1986) suggests, is a fragile basis on which to found theories of identity. Liegeois does provide a more flexible view of those placed in the category of Gypsy than Clebert (1963), seeing them as a grouping with a diverse range of social, political, cultural, and ethnic origins, but his position ties him to the diversity-equals-unity analysis that Acton (1974) and, among other analysts of the American situation, Hancock (1987) promote. This latter relationship, which appears to be a trans-Atlantic mutual reinforcement-appreciation pact, seems to have caused understanding of the American Gypsy population to be ossified in a cryogenic capsule dating from some puerile, early-nineteenth-century wasteland of reductionism: the world is viewed through the tight aperture of the eugenic gaze.

Okely makes the point, like Liegeois (1986), that Gypsy identity is amorphous. In common with Acton (1974) and Hancock (1987) in the American context, she sees the groups that constitute the Gypsy population as having a range and mixture of backgrounds. In her second chapter, "Modern Misrepresentations," she suggests that Gypsies have been portrayed as "victims of cultural disintegration" (1983, 28). She argues that they are not a separate or complete cultural group. For her, Gypsies have changed with the dominant order, in that they are and have been connected to and are interdependent with the wider economy. This, according to Okely, is exemplified by the presence of rural and nonrural groups of Gypsies. Although Okely represents a soft position, relative to Clebert (1963) and Acton (1974), she continues to portray Traveler identity as a collective connected by difference, a contradiction that does not help in terms of making her analysis more acceptable to the discerning reader.

Hawes and Perez also argue that Gypsies have "never constituted a homogenous group" (1995, 7) and that "they are a most disunited and ill-defined people" (1995, 7). Taking the lead from Acton (1974), they see Gypsies as possessing a "continuity rather than a community of culture" (1995, 7). They support Liegeois (1986), seeing Gypsies as "a whole, whose component features are linked to one another; a structure that is not rigid but ever-changing." Hawes and Perez continue:

The Irish Travelers in particular, whose Celtic origins and background to some extent set them at odds with the rest, are nevertheless so closely identified, interbred, and integrated with the Gypsies, over at least two hundred years, that their experience is directly related to our purposes. (1995, 7)

Historical evidence makes it hard to ignore the potential admixture of Gypsy origins. Hawes and Perez state:

We may guess at the many social and economic pressures which could have driven previously settled people to take up life on the road in those times, no doubt to add to the numberless peddlers, hawkers, vagrants, and beggars which made up the Elizabethan underclass. (1995, 7)

Hawes and Perez (1995), in suggesting that there have been constant additions to Gypsy populations from the settled community over time, make it difficult to sustain a notion of a traditional blood lineage of Gypsies. On the contrary, their position does seem to support the probability that Gypsies are essentially a social phenomenon rather than a biologically ethnic or racial type. As a consequence this, together with other considerations presented in this chapter, casts all sorts of doubts on the true identity of those individuals and groups seen to be Gypsies that have arrived in the Americas from the earliest colonial times.

Hawes and Perez (1995) do not clearly articulate or establish the relationship that Gypsies have to wider social considerations because the social reality and origin of Gypsies are not translated. Their argument is vague in terms of the social generation of the Gypsy population, and, in effect, this promotes a notion of a collective origin of the group. The analysis follows the tendency of the romantic tradition established by other writers, for example Hancock (1987) and Kenrick and Clark (1995), who suggest that the Gypsy population is the result of family, blood, or even tribal lineage. A position of this type allows such writers to theoretically champion an oppressed ethnic group and fight the cause of minority rights, but it obscures other possible forms of group generation arising out of the relationship between the Gypsy population and social phenomena affecting a much wider constituency.

Sutherland's position (1975), which she later develops (1986), demonstrates the omnipotence of this romantic perspective that seems related to the wish for a mysterious collectivity of Gypsies. She looks at the social, political, and ceremonial patterns of groups of Travelers in the United States (in particular around the town of Barvale, California). She applies the Romany term *kumponia* to these activities and interactions. In her effort to uncover the economic organization of "Rom in America" (1975, 38), she refers to a number of formally traveling family groups under the collective name of "Rom." Like other writers (some using the other generic labels—Gypsy or Traveler, for example), she deploys this as an umbrella term for varying collections of current and former nomadic peoples, including Machwaya, Mikailesti, and Gurkwe. She provides no explanation for her rationale, other than seeing the connections between the lifestyles she describes as evidence of this ethnic typology.

Most of the people Sutherland (1975) writes about were not full-time nomads, although constant and consistent traveling interspersed by short to long sedentary living was not uncommon (families spent between 6 and 66 percent of their time traveling; 15). Sutherland goes on to look at economic relations between these groups and between the whole category of Rom and non-Gypsies, including welfare considerations.

Gypsy Work

The main weakness of Sutherland's analysis is that what is being portrayed is a group of families that have either carried nomadic traditions from their East European origins or adopted this way of life since arriving in the United States. The exact character of traveling genealogy is not examined, so these customs may be socially adopted and not necessarily be part of a biological inheritance handed down through a blood lineage. The basic connection between these groups is their background as traveling people. Their customs, traditions, and economic structures have no necessary Rom cultural or ethnic bias. Sutherland

(1975) does not seem to see the possibility that the cultural and economic ways of the community she examines could emanate from a shared (not necessarily related to Rom ways) lifestyle connected with a migrant background as much as from a cultural tradition set in an ethnic framework of Romhood. This can be seen from Sutherland's critique of Clebert's (1963) attempt to identify Gypsy occupational categories, like musicians or metalworkers. In short, she argues that Rom have a very wide range of economic relations, proposing that the basic tenet of these relations is cooperation between Rom for the exploitation of non-Gypsies (Sutherland 1975, 22). She gives little consideration to the possibility that this occupational network may not be culturally rooted or connected to an ethnic mechanism, but rather may be generated by prevailing material and social conditions, which may conscript as well as shed personnel (which might result in the expansion, contraction, and cultural and ethnic diversity of what is seen as the Rom population).

I have found this process exemplified in my own experience on a number of occasions. While on a poor run of luck or judgment (depending on the way one looks at it), I supplemented my gaming career, taking a job working on crash-damaged cars in Orlando. The employment didn't really suit me, or rather I didn't suit it; so my hiring could be seen as a type of charitable act on the part of my boss, a man I had been put in touch with by an associate in my track craft. However, I think I offered a counseling option to a number of disgruntled car owners bewailing their need of my employer's services, many of them curious about my accent. One day I found myself talking to an eighty-two-year-old woman who called herself Jemmy. She told me:

> *The Tinkers used to do all this type of work. They were real good at it too. But the Tinkers have all gone. Their place has been taken by kids working through college, or trailer trash.*

I told her I was from a Gypsy background, and she said:

> *So this stuff must be in your blood, . . . You're probably naturally good at metalwork and such.*

However, as a metalworker I provoked more sympathy than adulation from my colleagues, most of whom at that time were of Puerto Rican origin. I talked to my boss about Jemmy's theory, and he agreed that after World War II, Gypsies had a reputation for metalwork in the area; he had gone into the business working for Gypsies, but most of those families had made money and had gone into car sales. This all seemed very approximate, and what could be said was limited to there being a shift in the background of metalworking personnel in the district.

Ascript Me Not

The unproblematic connection between ethnicity and behavior is taken up by others (A. and F. Rehfisch 1975; Barth 1975; parts of Kornblum 1975; Guy 1975; Okely 1975). For example, Miller (1975, 41) examines what she calls the "American Rom," specifically focusing on an "ideology of defilement." But, again, the basic weakness in this premise is that it assumes that various groups of nomadic people are a homogenous ethnic category—Rom. The flaws in this argument are highlighted by Guy (1975, 221–22) when he acknowledges, "how Roms should be characterized is a basic problem." He goes on to point to the confusion among

> *social anthropologists who have pursued an inconclusive search for definitive objective criteria of the ethnic group.*

He cites the attack made by Barth (1970) on this whole approach. For Barth,

> *the ascriptive aspect is logically prior to any objective characteristics of the ethnic group.* (quoted by Guy 1975, 222)

This position seems to indicate that there is a propensity among social anthropologists to *create* ethnic types on the basis of certain observed characteristics that appear to have similar elements. Thus, it could, in terms of Gypsies, be argued that itinerancy is an ascriptive aspect, which exists prior to the anthropologist labeling it as an objective characteristic. The possibility that a range of people, from varying backgrounds and ethnic groups, could live a nomadic lifestyle is not addressed, especially if they can be described as carrying other ascriptive aspects (for example, employment; see Okely 1983, 49–65) that in turn become objective characteristics. These other ascriptive aspects may have more to do with mobile living than any ethnic propensities. This possibility is not considered.

In contrast Kornblum, looking at Boyash Gypsies, notes that one family, the Ivanoviches, although not Gypsies, maintain a nomadic style of existence:

> *Their family economy and their relations with other groups in the camp are very much grounded in the rootlessness and disruption.* (1975, 131)

This brings them to adopt Gypsy ways:

> *In consequence they often have need of advice and material support which the Gypsies are in a position to provide.* (1975, 131)

Kornblum noted certain ascriptive aspects that correspond to the objective characteristics of Gypsy lifestyle, but saw that this did not automatically lead to being part of a Gypsy category. This conclusion was based on the relative comfort expressed or observed among non-Gypsy migrants and Gypsies. Although an entire catalog of ascriptive aspects might have been fulfilled by this family, the rather abstract and vague notion of comfort excluded them from being seen or portrayed as Gypsies. For Kornblum, the Ivanoviches' relative discomfort with a traveling lifestyle showed them to be involved in a temporary response to their economic and social circumstances and did not express a permanent ethnic or genealogical propensity.

Willems argues that

> *As a rule Gypsy specialists concentrate on striking likenesses and have a far less keen eye for differences. . . . This fixation on the supposed*

uniqueness of Gypsies has meant that no comparative studies of people in roughly the same circumstances were forthcoming. (1997, 298–99)

His conclusion, when discussing Dutch Travelers, is not too far from Kornblum's:

When, several years ago, a colleague of mine in the company of British anthropologist Judith Okely visited a caravan camp in Leiden, they saw parallels with British and Irish Gypsy-Travelers. They knew for certain that these were Gypsies. The Dutch women living in the caravans, however, were having none of it and stressed that they were native Dutch. That social surroundings can, as it were, compel people to behave in a certain way is something that Gypsy specialists do not acknowledge sufficiently. (1975, 299)

Willems goes on to demonstrate the prevalence of this type of analysis:

The writers of an analysis of the begging of Gypsies in seventeenth-century western Europe omit to mention that at the time the number of beggars was, in any event, large. Elaborate discussions of the deceptions perpetrated by Gypsies throughout the German countryside in the eighteenth century lose much of their ethnic charge if we realize that a legion of drifters struggled to extract themselves from the swamp of poverty through ruses and tricks. (1975, 299)

Of course, many of these groups and individuals may have found themselves transported to America as Gypsies (see chapter 4).

The totality of the analysis in Rehfisch (1975) suggests that while there may be some consistent patterns of activity among groups of Gypsies, it demonstrates that there is no overriding connection between the very disparate groups that make up the category, apart from the need, wish, or obligation to travel; and even this is questionable, as Guy (1975, 202) points out. This could link Gypsies to Bedouins, Bushmen, Aborigines, Inuits, and some Native American groups: any and all of the world's itinerant peoples. Are they all Gypsies? It can be seen that there has been a failure on the part of writers on Gypsy issues to explicate the Gypsy population as a distinct group based on tradition, habit, or lifestyle; this might go to some way toward explaining why Gypsy identity relies so heavily on forms of self-ascription, the problems of which have been reflected on above.

This propensity has a history. As Willems explains:

> *The notion of a Gypsy people has become dominant, and other group categories such as pilgrims, spies, criminal vagabonds, heathens and the mixed category of social outsiders has faded into the background.* (1997, 301)

Here Willems points to a historical process that has merged various traveling groups into one all-embracing category—Gypsies. Many of these itinerant groups traveled for economic reasons rather than an ethnic drive or a racial urge. These groups would have included showpeople, weavers, landless laborers, knife-sharpeners, drovers, beggars (see also Mayall 1988, 1995), and, yes, gamblers. The ascriptive aspect (traveling), although existing prior to categorization by writers on Gypsy issues, has been used by the same to define all these groups under one ethnic label.

Although it may be important for individual and group identity to emphasize various ethnic boundaries, tastes, styles, and so on, the effort to seek to identify habits or defining traditions or traits on behalf of a particular group, which merely distinguishes or categorizes, seems highly questionable in terms of its political or social motives. The practice of aggregation of Gypsy identity is an underlying theme in the literature (see, for example, Hancock 1987; Kenrick and Clark 1995; Kenrick and Bakewell 1990). This kind of perspective risks amounting to little more than a subtle form of discrimination. A human being categorized as a Gypsy has a logical social place and even a physical locale, such as the site in Europe, maybe a trailer park, or a particular district in the United States (as, under the South African apartheid regime, blacks belonged on a Bantu reservation, and, at one time, Native Americans were corralled on reservations).

The practice of defining Gypsy characteristics from a very broad lifestyle basis and what is a diverse collection of people, and from a range of social, ethnic, and cultural backgrounds (see Lucassen et al. 1998; Willems 1997), might be likened to the claims about white racial tradition or ethnically black behavior. Such distinctions are racist in themselves in that they fail to consider, and in effect deny the existence of, the wide and varied nature of cultural traditions and ethnic identities within the very limited taxonomy of color. It is valuable to ask what purpose there is in labeling uniquely Gypsy behavior or ways (see Hancock, Dowd, and Djuric 1998, for example). How could such distinctions have anything other than extremely limited applicability in a multiracial, multiethnic, cross-cultural society? Although this book cannot be totally effective in terms of addressing this propensity, it is hoped that it will stand as a question mark over this theme that runs through most of the literature pertaining to Gypsies.

For Willems (1997), the character of Gypsy identity has been obfuscated by the nature of research into Gypsy identity (most of the writers critically assessed in this book have been affected by this). Willems notes how the early writers interested in Gypsies collected historical and mythological fragments relating to a range of itinerant groups. From this somewhat random collage they developed a Gypsy racial history and identity. According to Willems, writers like Fraser have followed and built on this foundation. When, as might be expected, no true Gypsy type can be identified that corresponds to this primal model (for example, Nazi research of the early 1940s traced family lines going back several generations but could find no conclusive evidence of a Gypsy lineage; see Willems 1997, 29), it is concluded that this category has disappeared, having been integrated and/or assimilated to a greater or lesser extent according to the level they correspond to the ideal.

Although Willems, alongside Lucassen and Cottaar (1998), later strongly implies that Gypsy populations are socially generated phenomena, made up by a variety of ethnic types brought together (for academic and juridical inspection only) by sociohistorical forces, including the rise of nationalism (Willems 1997, 22–24), he does not elaborate on the underlying social forces that can give rise to the creation of or conscription to an ethnicity. Neither does he postulate, in any definite manner, possible external binding factors between groups identified as Gypsies. These issues will be addressed in chapter 5.

Conclusion

In this chapter, I have looked at the nature of American Gypsy studies and how this has been influenced by—and to a huge extent replicates—European perspectives. Within this, I critique the notion of Gypsy ethnicity as developed in the literature focusing on Gypsy identity. I have pointed out the limitations of the literature, highlighting the overall failure to frame a sociological ethos within the research and, as such, a failure to consider the social context within which the Gypsy population has developed. This included consideration of sea Gypsy and snowbird lifestyles to problematize by comparison the dominant presentation of the ethnic Gypsy. The critique of this propensity within theories surrounding Gypsies is founded on the literature's habit of portraying Gypsy identity as a racial or ethnic category based on a paradigm of romanticism. I show that by way of subjective and irrational forms of self-ascription and fragile language links, a spurious biological, hereditary nexus is erected that in effect facilitates the bypassing of consideration of a social dimension to this identity.

Within and throughout the analysis presented in this chapter, the contradictory proposal that runs through the literature is made manifest: groups of itinerant people are a homogenous population made up of heterogeneous groups. I have shown that although this constructed homogeneity has been challenged in recent times (Willems 1997; Lucassen 1998), it continues to dominate the discourse surrounding Gypsy identity and is the foundation on which the claim of difference and the assumption of Gypsy ethnicity are premised.

The chapter finishes by questioning the purpose of the effort to identify and categorize Gypsies and, laying the ground for chapter 5, identifies the paucity of an analysis within the literature concerned with Gypsies of the possible social structural bonding agents of the diversity of people that might be labeled the Gypsy population.

4

Historical Genesis of American Gypsies

In chapters 2 and 3, it has been argued via an analysis of social situations and narrative exploration that the labeling of American Gypsies as a race, an ethnicity, or even a homogeneous cultural group is an inappropriate, illogical, and morally questionable enterprise. In this chapter, I will look at the historical evidence of a Gypsy presence in the United States and question this as verification of the existence of an ethnic, racial, or cultural American Gypsy population.

Transportation: The Dubious Seed of the American Gypsy Population

Brown (1929, 148) makes the case for an early Gypsy presence in the United States. He quotes a Gypsy who told him that his great-uncle fought in the American Revolution in 1776. Paine, in his *History of East Harwich*, refers to a Gypsy family living at Grassy Pond during the mid-1700s (Paine 1937, 464). The practice of the transportation of Gypsies from Europe during the colonial period is used to substantiate these assertions of a primal Gypsy presence in the United States (Brown 1922, 16; see also Coelho 1892).

Most writers on American Gypsies in the contemporary era (for example, Vaux de Foletier 1970, 13–22; Gropper 1975, 17) have followed earlier writers with regard to the origins of the Gypsy population of the United States, seeing the deportations in the colonial times, from in particular Britain and to a lesser extent France, Portugal, and Spain, as the genesis of the Gypsy population in the New World. For instance, Hall has pointed out that Gypsy names were commonly found on British transportation lists between 1787 and 1867 (G. Hall 1915, 281). However, Hall (and by association Hancock 1987, who calls on Hall to support his position) is undermined by a seeming lack of basic general knowledge (and perhaps is urged by wish fulfillment); British transportation to America effectively ended in 1783 after the War of Independence. It can only be conjectured that the names that Hall identified were in fact dispatched to Australia.

Sway (1988) cites evidence of Gypsies in colonial America by way of the 1695 legal proceedings against a woman named Joane Scot. The court record, filed in Henrico County, Virginia, on February 1, 1695, stated that

> *Joane Scot is dischard from ye p'sentim'ts of the Grand Jury. It being the opinion of this Court that ye Act against ffornication does not touch her (she) being an Egyptian and a non-Christian woman.*

However, Sway goes on to argue that further evidence suggests that not only were there Gypsies living in colonial America, but that also groups of Gypsies encountered hostility from colonial settlers. Her rather confusing account further asserts (1988, 37–39) that less than two hundred years after the Gypsies arrived in western Europe, anti-Gypsy activity had reached highly threatening levels and that by the end of the seventeenth century all the nations of Europe with New-World holdings were deporting Gypsies or people who were called or known as Gypsies.

The analysis that Sway and Hall (and Hancock) present might be seen as indicative of the understanding of the origins of American Gypsies. It appears that those who contended that the existence of a Gypsy population of the United States can be premised on the seedbed of seventeenth- and eighteenth-century penal transportation are guilty of the same type of ragged and doubtful scholarship that, with a few exceptions (Mayall, Willems, Lucassen et al.), runs throughout the literature focusing on Gypsies. A more careful examination of penal transportation demonstrates the implausibility that this practice might have fueled the generation of the American Gypsy population.

Non-British Transportation

There are records of groups, named as Gypsies, being transported from Germany to the German colony in Pennsylvania (Shoemaker 1926, 4) and of French initiatives that include a two-year period between 1801 and 1803 when Napoleon Bonaparte transported hundreds of individuals labeled as Gypsies, mostly men, to Louisiana. However, after Bonaparte sold the Louisiana territory to President Jefferson in 1803, much of the French Gypsy deportation strategy was halted (Vaux de Foletier 1970, 13–22). Likewise, Spain and Portugal instigated deportations below the equator, and in the sixteenth century Portugal sent hundreds of individuals labeled as Gypsies to Brazil (Coelho 1892, 79–86). At the same time, Spain was deporting people designated as Gypsies to its South American colonies (*Journal of the Gypsy Lore Society* 1892, 61).

For all this, I will concentrate on the character of British penal transportation to America, not only because it is seen in the literature as the main root of the Gypsy population of the United States, but also because the British record of transportation to America covers a longer historical period and is more detailed, accessible, and reliable relative to other colonial powers of the time.

British Transportation

The transportation of British convicts was, historically, a worldwide phenomenon; convicts were sent from Britain to America, the Caribbean, and Australia. In America, the transported ran the risk of being sold into slavery, and of those that were sent to Australia many were forced to fend for themselves and eke out an existence in penal colonies. By 1772, 60 percent of all male convicts in England were being transported. By 1775, only 10 percent of felons served prison sentences. After America won independence from Britain in 1783, these statistics began to reverse, and by the 1790s imprisonment accounted for two-thirds of criminal sentences.

Convicts were the second-largest body of immigrants to be compelled to go to America. They were only outnumbered by African slaves. The legal structure for this banishment was provided by the Transportation Act of 1718. During the period of British transportation to America around fifty-two thousand convicts were exiled, about eight hundred per year.

In the main, transportation was a punishment for property offenses; it was often used to punish those found guilty of lesser capital offenses, such as stealing sheep and petty theft. The most common offense among the transported was grand larceny—theft of goods valued at a shilling and above. In addition to ordinary criminals, Irish courts also banished large numbers of those labeled vagabonds. Transportation was used as an alternative form of capital punishment to the death sentence; like hanging, it was a primary penalty. However, penal banishment was often no more than a slow alternative to a fast death. Many convicts were unable to survive the harshness of the journey across the Atlantic, and of those who did many perished not long after disembarkation, either by way of the work demanded of them or sickness.

Transportation Prior to the 1718 Transportation Act

Simson maintains that Gypsy transportation to America from England, Wales, Scotland, and Ireland started as early as the settlement period of the 1600s. Individuals and groups could be transported if they were seen to be by habit and repute Gypsies (1865, 418). The earliest documentation of a Gypsy presence in America dates from the time of the administration of Richard Cromwell (the Lord Protector, Oliver's political successor and son). The first trans-Atlantic expulsions of Gypsies were initiated in the form of the 1661 Commissions and Instructions that were issued to justices and constables by Act of Parliament and that provided them the means to arrest those labeled Gypsies. This legislation was framed at a time when the wandering poor of Britain were becoming a problematic group, one of constant concern to the political establishment. These waves of landless laborers, which had been growing from the first vibrations of the agricultural enclosure movement, begged a solution of the British ruling classes.

As such, the history of transportation can be seen to be more than a chronicle of punishment. Penal servitude was also an economic tool, a means of ridding Britain of nonproductive labor after the beginnings of industrialization and a way of relocating redundant agricultural labor to colonial locations where it was required. Many of the transported would have been forced into temporary or even perpetual servitude (MacRitchie 1894, 102), slaves in all but name.

It is likely that many people transported from England as Gypsies during the second half of the seventeenth century were taken to the labor-thirsty British plantations in Jamaica and Barbados, with no more than a relatively few getting to the agricultural estates of Virginia. However, the existence of a record of Gypsy transportation, particularly in the very early period of British penal transportation to America, is not sufficient to conclude that those so removed were in fact ethnically Gypsy. For example, a reference of November 1665 comments upon the motives for indenturing so-called Gypsies and others:

> *The light regard paid to the personal right of individuals was shown by a wholesale deportation of poor people at this time to the West Indies . . . out of a desire as weel to promote the Scottish and English plantations in Gemaica and Barbadoes for the honour of their country, as to free the kingdom of the burden of many strong and idle beggars, Egyptians, common and notorious thieves, and other dissolute and looss persons banished and stigmatised for gross crimes.* (Chambers 1858, 304)

In 1714, British merchants and planters applied to the Privy Council for permission to ship Gypsies to the Caribbean to be used as slaves (MacRitchie 1894). According to a document dated January 1, 1715, "Prisoners . . . were sentenced . . . to be transported to the plantations for being [by] habit and repute gipsies" (*Memorabilia* 1835, 424–26). The legal definition of a Gypsy throughout this period in England included "all such persons not being Fellons wandering and pretending [i.e., identifying themselves to be Egypcians, or wandering in the Habite, Forme or Attyre] counterfayte Egypcians" (Statutes, 39 *Eliz.*, c.4, quoted in Smith 1971, 109. See also Axon 1897 and Beier 1985, 58–62). This, of course, is an arbitrary definition and as such does not provide definitive evidence of a Gypsy racial type or ethnic lineage.

Following the trans-Atlantic crossing, any notion of Gypsy identity seemed to largely evaporate. For example, whether destined for Virginia, Jamaica, or elsewhere, the first port of call for huge numbers of those taken from Britain to America was Barbados, a major entrepôt for slave distribution to British colonies in the western hemisphere at the time (Hancock 1980). However, as Hancock (1987) points out, while the designations "Gypsy, Gypcian, Egyptian, &c." turn up in the records of transportation located in Britain, nothing similar appears anywhere in the documents in Barbados. Hancock goes on to point out that local censuses do not mention Gypsies; however, Jews are listed separately from other whites (Dunn 1962).

Although Handler (1970, 127) states that Amerindian slaves brought in from South America and possibly New England were also not listed, this does not explain why there is no trace of a Gypsy presence in the census record. Hancock provides a number of possible excuses for this lack:

1. Gypsies may have been counted together with the white population, perhaps because of their common origin at time of shipment, and as such were not officially registered separately.
2. Gypsies were shipped on to the North American colonies, but did not stay in the West Indies long enough to gain recognition as a definite racial or ethnic group.
3. Some Gypsies returned to Britain, while interbreeding made those that stayed increasingly less distinct.

However, it seems doubtful that any of the above adequately justifies almost complete omission of Gypsies as an ethnic or racial category among those transported, particularly given the very emotive labeling of this group and the fact that being part of the same might be the sole reason for individual or group rejection from British society.

Even if one ignored the financial and political expedience of applying the label of Gypsy to nuisance groups sent to America in the late seventeenth and early eighteenth centuries and just accepted that those categorized were in fact Gypsies, the earliest years of transportation, the period prior to the early 1700s, would have been a relative trickle in comparison to the movement from Britain to America after 1718.

Transportation from 1718 to 1783

During the later (and main) period of transportation from Britain to America, the most usual destinations were Maryland and Virginia. The occupational profile of those sentenced to transportation covered a broad spectrum, although on arrival many of them were bought into servitude or taken on as servants. Transportees could be sold to private employers, mostly middle-size plantation owners. The price of a British convict was only about 30 percent of what might be expected for an African slave, probably because the British were seen to be relatively idle and were said to have complained more than their African counterparts.

Although transportation was the most common punishment for children, as it ostensibly spared their lives, more than half those transported were in their twenties, many just into the third decade of their existence. Around 80 percent of those transported were male. Women were treated more leniently by courts and were usually not involved in serious crimes. As such, the argument for transportation as the foundation of the American Gypsy population was undermined almost from the start, given that it was likely that the transported males who were able to procreate would have, at best, only a 25 percent chance of maintaining an unsullied gene pool.

The transportation sentences were for seven years, fourteen years, or life in exile. The total number of convicts transported to America from England and Wales was nearly thirty-five thousand. Ireland transported about sixteen thousand convicts, and Scotland approximately eight hundred.

So more than 67 percent of British convicts transported to America came from English origins, sentenced in English courts. These figures reflect the differences in the population sizes of the nations that made up Britain and their rates of crime. London had the highest crime rate in Britain, so by far the largest number of those transported came from the expanding city sprawl of the capital of empire, which was not the understood habitat of the rurally situated, roving Gypsy.

Given the overall profile of those transported it seems that colonial transportation from Britain is a fragile basis on which to build the foundation of the American Gypsy population. By association it is likely that the problems associated with taking British transportation of Gypsies as part of the genesis of the contemporary Gypsy population of the United States would be equally applicable in terms of other colonial powers. However, even if this were not the case, the notion of the establishment of a Gypsy bloodline in the New World has other flaws. Burnett, who believed that the ancestors of the Melungeons of Tennessee may have entered the country as Portuguese or Gypsies, suggests that "some families may have intermingled with the negroes or Indians or both" (1889, 349). It would be surprising, if such intermingling were not a widespread phenomenon, that the course of a quarter of a millennium (or six generations between then and now) would not seriously threaten any notion of a surviving Gypsy race or ethnicity.

Advance Australia Fair

There is a further illogicality of the transportation genesis position. After America gained independence, Britain began to send her convicts to penal colonies in Australia. On May 13, 1787, the First Fleet set sail for Australia. It consisted of six ships carrying 717 convicts, 48 of whom died on the way. They disembarked in Port Jackson in January 1788, after deciding that their first choice Botany Bay, was unsuitable.

The period of British transportation to Australia, between 1787 and 1868, was almost sixteen years (20 percent) longer than the period of British transportation to America. During this period, 158,702 convicts were sent to Australia from England and Ireland and 1,321 from the rest of the British Empire, in the region of 2,000 per annum, more than twice the annual figures for British transportation to America during the eighteenth century. Of course, the future impact of an early Gypsy influx should have been greater in Australia relative to the United States, given the much smaller population pool. If transportation is taken as a viable foundation for contemporary Gypsy populations, it is surprising, given the above analysis, that American assertions of the same are much more vociferous than are calls for recognition of an Australian Gypsy population, which are noticeable by their scarcity in the literature. I suggest that this comparison, alongside the preceding analysis of transportation from Britain to America, demonstrates that the idea that the Gypsy population of the United States might be the progeny of transportation is ill informed if not indefensibly spurious.

Were the Gypsies Really Gypsies?

The upheavals that shook and shaped Europe between the eighteenth and nineteenth centuries, up to, including, and beyond the liberal period of mass immigration into the United States between 1845 and 1870, would certainly have had an effect on the numbers of people adopting or being forced into an itinerant lifestyle. For example, in Britain from the latter part of the enclosure period to the English Bourgeois Revolution (the Civil War) and right through to the later stages of the Industrial Revolution, an appreciable section of the British population would have been uprooted. A significant number of people might have been obliged to take up what might be seen as Gypsy habits and therefore become Gypsies by repute. In Britain, groups of unemployed laborers and the lower echelons of royal patronage and the aristocratic system would have been displaced from the mid-1600s. It is also possible that transportation of those labeled Gypsy across the empire could have provided a convenient means of disposing of those who may have proved problematic to the English or British state from Cromwell to the Victorian era, and other European regimes may well have followed or replicated the example.

There is a long history of large numbers of rovers or wayfarers (see Jusserand 1961; Mayall 1988), including out-of-bond peasants, performers, peddlers, pilgrims, mendicant friars, and preachers. The literature relating to Gypsies acknowledges the presence of Tinkers before any records relating to Gypsies (or Egyptians—as exotic wanderers were known) appeared (see Acton 1974, 66, for example). Shakespeare's *Henry IV* refers to Tinkers—a common surname and trade name in the 1300s (*Oxford English Dictionary*). In Britain, from the twelfth century onward, groups of people, who were taken to be of foreign origin, were recorded as earning a living from any number of occupations, from casual agricultural labor to fortune-telling. This was long before such groups were considered to be of a specific type or race (see Mayall 1988). In the mid-1300s, there was a growing number of rovers, a wandering class of serfs or escaped villains (Statute of Labourers 1351, cited in Jusserand 1961, 144–48). While English law prohibited people from leaving their home districts, landowners sought out day and wage laborers (Jusserand 1961, 144–48), encouraging the generation of a mobile workforce.

By the fifteenth century, Europe had a massive itinerant population that could be considered to be part of the roots of the modern proletariat. As Okely (1983, 14) suggests, this group may have been the ancestors of many Gypsies: those who were not bound as serfs or assimilated into guilds or trades. It seems likely that if there was any Gypsy presence in the early years of American history it was made up of some of the successors of these European wanderers (see Nemeth 2002, for example). These individuals and groups, in common with the escaped villains and rovers, sold their labor at a daily or hourly rate (Mandel 1979, 34).

Okely (1983, 14) notes that Marx suggests another origin of the modern proletariat that could also have some relationship to the contemporary Gypsy population—a section of the population that spurned the wage labor:

> The prelude of the revolution that laid the foundation of the capitalist mode of production was played in the last third of the fifteenth and first decade of the sixteenth century. A mass of free proletarians was hurled on the labour market by the breaking up of the bands of feudal retainers. (1887, 718)

Former clerks, servants to the feudal nobility, became wandering beggars. Dispossessed peasants may also have added to the groups that were to be called Gypsy, when their land was no longer agriculturally cultivated but instead turned into grazing for sheep during the growth in the wool industry (see Mandel 1979, 35).

It is credible that many from these groups—that amounted to a mass of free labor—may have, by association and marriage, become known as, or, for various social or economic reasons, called themselves Egyptians and eventually Gypsies. Throughout Europe, as Clebert (1967, 63) notes, the appearance of exotic traveling groups coincided with the establishment of the "corporations de gueuserie," the "guilds of beggars." While it may have been that groups of beggars, alien travelers, or entertainers had various origins and backgrounds, they could also have been different representations of the same phenomenon. Even if this were not the case, people may have moved between such groups without undermining the ascribed and organizational boundaries (see Barth 1969). Okely argues that these itinerant groups, made up mainly of indigenous, disenfranchised individuals, may well have come together for reasons of survival and could have "adopted an exotic nomenclature, parts of a second secret language" (1983, 15). This would have been adventageous for gaining certain types of work or even earning income as entertainers or traveling performers.

The circumstances surrounding a Gypsy identity that appears to have been, to a great extent, erroneously cobbled together via a complexity of social, political, and economic considerations from the British agricultural revolution on, together with the character of transportation, seem to seriously undermine (at least) the proposal that an ethnically Gypsy population in the United States has a clear historical lineage in America, following a path from Europe and perhaps subcontinental origins.

Migration

As penal transportation is unable to offer an adequate or credible base for the current Gypsy population of the United States, straightforward migration might be looked to as a means to substantiate claims for an early Gypsy presence in America. However, the controls on immigration during the major period of European migration to America were relatively stringent. It was far from the informal and anonymous process that is sometimes portrayed.

It took until the late 1820s for the annual number of immigrants to America to exceed the ten thousand mark. Up to this point, there is a great deal of commentary that suggests that there was no Gypsy presence from the first centuries of American colonization. For instance, Hoyland points out that one of the earliest analysts of Gypsies—Grellmann—was of the opinion that America is the only part of the world in which Gypsies are not known (1816, 11), and Crabb claimed that there were no Gypsies on the American continent during the colonial period (1831, 6). Contemporary writers have reinforced this position; for example, Salo has argued that the Romnichels began appearing in the United States in the 1850s (1982, 281). Establishing the likelihood of a Gypsy presence in the colonial and immediate postcolonial period in American history is complicated by the fact that there is no solid indication of reliable means of, or attempts at, establishing exactly what constituted a Gypsy in Europe between the 1600s and the mid- to late nineteenth century.

Prerevolution Migration

Britain, especially England, underwent its first great age of migration from 1600 to 1800, when huge numbers of people left for America and the Caribbean. The destinations and the composition of emigrant groups varied, as did their motives for leaving Great Britain. During the seventeenth century, around four hundred thousand English and Irish settlers immigrated to America, the majority bound for the expanding English plantations. Though this was a massive movement of labor, it was essential for the development of staple agriculture (sugar, tobacco) in the West Indies and the Chesapeake Bay region. In the plantation colonies, the demand for labor was enormous.

However, movement between Britain and America was restricted by the twin obstacles of distance and money. There were a limited number of ways in which these barriers could be overcome: Paying one's own passage was likely feasible to only the fairly well-off tradesmen, small businessmen, or farmers. The other means included finding an employer in America willing to sponsor one's passage or take one on in indentured service. Before the American Revolution, indentured servants (including convicts) comprised the majority of emigrants from the British Isles. They were mostly contracted to work in tobacco and sugar fields, the majority committing themselves to between four and seven years of labor in return for their passage to America, board, and freedom dues. However, throughout the prerevolutionary period the proportion of men coming from Britain to America from skilled and semiskilled backgrounds rose steadily, while the number of servants from unskilled work or those registered without a designated occupation fell. This prerevolutionary trend shows the class profile of individuals arriving in America from Britain moving from the working class to the lower-middle class. At the same time, an increase in the volume of trade and the expansion of the territory brought with it a growing number of young men from the upper and upper-middle classes who moved to the colonies to work in trade and business or to take up posts in the military and in government service. Yet again, this goes against the notion of transportation providing a credible basis for the current Gypsy population of America. While there would certainly have been some skilled tradesmen within the British Gypsy population, those designated as Gypsy within the British context were usually associated with the lower ranks of society.

This being the case, it is very difficult to see how the majority of British Gypsies might have arranged passage to the New World at that time, given prohibitive costs and the likelihood of a commitment of indenture that does not fit understood Gypsy cultural attitudes.

The period after 1760 saw an increasing number of skilled and independent migrants who deliberately choose to emigrate against a background of growing prosperity and trade. The main reasons for this mass movement, especially in the eighteenth century, were the increasingly complex global economy and the search for new commercial outlets.

Postrevolution Migration

After 1783, following the American War of Independence, the movement from Britain to North America rose sharply. Indentured servitude continued to be a major consideration: about half of the migrants to the United States after the colonial period, up to the early 1800s, went as indentured servants.

Up to the first part of the 1820s, the mass exodus was accepted by those who had been born in America, if somewhat grudgingly, as it enhanced the much-needed growth in population. Initially, most of the new Americans were English-speaking Protestants and as such assimilated. But as the numbers of Irish and European Catholics increased, tension mounted. Anxiety about cheap labor and the fear of papal influence gave rise to the Know-Nothing movement, a group of individuals who demanded tighter controls on immigration and naturalization.

The great burgeoning of immigration came in the 1840s and 1850s. Poor harvests drove people from Britain and Northern Europe, escaping hunger. These conditions produced homelessness and poverty, the great motivators of petty crime, taxing the very limited resources of penal institutions of the time, which like much of the social plant of Britain lagged behind the demands put on them by conditions. Between 1845 and 1860, over

3.5 million people arrived in the United States. This is the most likely period for the arrival in America of people who might have adopted or been obliged to adopt Gypsy lifestyles. However, between 1820 and 1860, the United States and Great Britain were locked tightly together by culture and economic growth. Social upheaval and economic privation, arising out of the repeal of Britain's protective Corn Laws, the potato famine, and technological dislocation, cannot explain the huge mid-century gush of British migration to America. It was not desperation and poverty that took the majority of immigrants across the Atlantic but energy, resolve, and aspiration of a better existence and the will of millions to improve their life chances and those of their families in what was literally the New World. Far and away, the majority of European immigrants to the United States at this time were aspiring and dynamic. This is evidenced by county histories, passenger lists of immigrant ships, census data, and manuscript collections in Britain and America. Such evidence demonstrates that after the initial settlements, people traveled to the United States in search of farm-land, education, employment, freedom to practice their religion, and to escape famine or war.

By the latter part of the nineteenth century, most of the people who left Britain to take up life in the United States were merchants, planters, field hands, or farmers or served with the great mercantile companies in the east. Many set up merchant houses, country stores, and plantations. There was also a flow of professional men and artisans (teachers, doctors, accountants, ministers, weavers, smiths, and carpenters). These were the middle and upper ranks of the lower classes. Immigrants still included those who could not afford the cost of passage, those desperate and poor from years of European food shortages and industrial depression. Yet those coming to the United States from Europe were, in the main, in search of opportunities rather than acting out of desperation. Most immigrants had something solid to offer the economy. There was no way through unless this was the case. Overall, analysis of migration patterns of this time does not seem to suggest the type of informal ethos of movement associated with Gypsy lifestyles.

Neither do the employment profiles associated with immigrants fit with those usually recognized as being part of a Gypsy existence.

After the first third of the nineteenth century, it seems the chances for establishing a viable basis for the current Gypsy population of America were low. At the same time, given the relatively low level of immigration prior to 1830, it seems erroneous to claim that Gypsy migration, a small proportion of even this relatively limited influx, is a feasible foundation for a distinct population the better part of two hundred years later. Even with the possible additions to the American Gypsy population via the slim window of liberal immigration attitudes between 1845 and 1870, which plunged newcomers into the seething cauldron of demographics and social interaction that the United States was at that period, such a proposition is less than convincing.

This being the case, it is likely that the white wanderers of America socially evolved from and out of the very solid mass of pragmatic labor that reached the shores of the United States in the second half of the nineteenth century and did not arrive ready made.

The Beginning of Official Immigration Controls

In 1870, about 12 percent of the United States' population had been born abroad, and this was the basis of the intense and wide opposition against free immigration. In response to continued protest, laws to regulate immigration were enacted. For instance, in 1882 the Chinese Exclusion Act put an end to the entry of all working-class Chinese. Later laws also barred people without adequate financial means, individuals with certain diseases, anarchists, and individuals who were diagnosed to be insane. The timing of immigration controls, together with contemporary popular feeling in the last part of the 1800s, suggests that there would have been little if any growth in the American Gypsy population via immigration in the late-nineteenth-century period.

Quota systems were introduced with the National Origins Acts of the 1920s. These quotas heavily favored British and northern European immigrants over those from southern and eastern Europe (Americans being at this time more accepting of the British and northern Europeans), the cultures and cheap labor of the Slavs, Greeks, Italians, and other southern and eastern Europeans being considered something of a threat. The quotas not only controlled what nationalities might enter the United States, but also barred entry to all but the most desirable and useful. In effect, the quotas would have made Gypsy entry into the United States difficult, to say the least. It is telling that Ellis Island did not recognize the category "Gypsy." The quotas remained in effect until 1965, when the government adjusted them to allow wider immigration from all countries into the United States.

Historical Foundations

It is purported that the historical foundation of American Gypsies through immigration or transportation from Europe was comprised of:

1. Gypsies who made up a proportion of the total numbers transported to the Americas during the colonial period (the keystone to the modern population hundreds of years later),

supplemented by:

2. Gypsies who entered the United States as members of the aspiring and dynamic masses, pre-1830,
3. a proportion of the European migrant population during the comparatively liberal period of immigration to the United States from 1845 to 1870 (this would appear to be very few going by contemporary sources. For example in 1874, the *American Cyclopaedia* argued that it was "questionable whether a band of genuine Gipsies has ever been in America"), and
4. Gypsies who managed to satisfy immigration requirements after 1880.

86 / Chapter 4

This is not convincing. The project to formulate a substantial concept of Gypsy roots, in an America set in the notion of blood or heritage, is deeply problematic.

From the cultural and biographical complexity of the European traveling population that existed before, during, and after the colonial period in America, it is possible to see the diverse social influences both within what might have been seen as the Gypsy population and between so-called Gypsies and non-Gypsies. It would seem likely that the history and lineage of Gypsies move across distinct borders and categories. This contrasts with the general portrayal of Gypsy lineage, history, and culture in the literature that in effect separates Gypsies into definite categories. For example, Earle et al. (1994) present the following table based on the five categories of Travelers outlined by the National Gypsy Council (NGC):

Table 3.1. Travelers Categorized

Tinkers	From Roman descent, skilled metalworkers with particular specialization in tools such as knives. The Industrial Revolution limited this trade, and many Tinkers moved on to scrap dealing.
Peddlers	Traveling salespeople providing any commodity required by outlying communities. Wares were also sold at fairs and markets, especially as the pottery industry expanded, so diversifying the range of goods.
Romanies	Probably descended from Indian nomadic tribes traveling across Europe in the fifteenth century. Although the language and nationality of the host country may have been superficially adopted, their culture remained separate. The Romany language, rooted in Sanskrit, is their own.
Irish Tinkers	People whose families traveled for centuries throughout Ireland, many of whom have been driven from the country by eviction, famine, and poverty. Their language is Gaelic based and called Shelta or Gammon. They have been joined recently by migrant Irishmen seeking construction work.
Scottish tinkers	Probably descended from Celtic metalworkers and originally called Tinkers. Their numbers were swelled by the massive Highland clearance campaigns of the nineteenth and early twentieth centuries. They are still more likely than other Travelers to use bender tents as homes.

It is difficult to claim that the groups identified within this categorization have stayed pure, and the NGC does note possible admixtures and the infiltration of the non-Gypsy community. However, other categories of Gypsy have been mooted: Push-rats, Mumpers, Pikies (Sandford 1973, 222), Didakais (Clebert 1964, 212), and Drovers (Toulson 1980). The Dublin Travellers Education and Development Group (DTEDG), although seeking to identify a distinct Traveler culture, points out the difficulties in establishing cultural purity, or definite distinctiveness:

> *customs, beliefs, and superstitions are shared with settled people. . . . This element of commonality of customs or pronunciation is worth pondering. . . . It simply reflects the close contact that the two cultures have had. There have been borrowings and leakages both ways. . . . In many examples of commonality it is, in fact, impossible to say which culture initiated the custom.* (DTEDG 1992, 12)

Noonan also confirms the probable complex nature of the development of the Irish Traveler population, stating that Travelers may be seen as:

> *the descendants of those people driven to the roads during times of economic and political turbulence in the seventeenth and nineteenth centuries.* (1994a, 5)

He goes on to point out that the various theories regarding Travelers' origins lack

> *conclusive evidence to support any single one of them.* (1994a, 5)

Social Generation versus Biological Heritage

By the mid- to late nineteenth century, the time most expedient for Gypsy entry to the United States, this group, the Gypsies, being a vast admixture of cultural influences and social and biological origins, was an established category in the European psyche. This picture of the cultural complexity of Gypsy identity further confirms the position that Gypsy populations are at least as much socially generated as they are biological or blood entities. As such, it cannot be taken for granted that individuals and groups who migrated or who were transported to the Americas from Britain and the rest of Europe were straightforwardly Gypsies. This, of course, problematizes the notion that they were the foundation of an American Gypsy population.

Alternative Foundations

Hancock (1987) argues that most American Gypsies are descended from the Gypsies freed from slavery in southeastern Europe between 1855 and 1864. For Sway (1988), it is difficult to determine what percentage of the contemporary Gypsy population living in the United States is descended from those labeled as Gypsies and deported to the Americas during colonial times. Based on information from her informants, Sway argues that the majority of American Gypsies are descended from immigrants who came to the United States during the large immigration of eastern Europeans in the late nineteenth century. However, the establishment of the basis of a Gypsy population in the United States would not have been helped by the development of entry procedures during the nineteenth century. In the latter half of the 1800s, Trigg notes that Gypsies from Slavic countries were arriving in the United States in appreciable numbers. However, by 1885 Gypsies were excluded by immigration policy, and many were returned to Europe (1973, 224). Benton's 1985 history of Ellis Island refers to massive deportations of Gypsies enacted by the United States Immigration Department authorities in 1905 and 1909, while Pitkin quotes from the *Tribune* of July 25th, 1909, which supported the upholding of the government's exclusion policy by Commissioner William Williams, who stated that

> *The whole country is better off without them, even though their wealth per capita was several times greater than the amount commonly required.* (Pitkin 1975, 60)

In fact, it is likely that Gypsy immigration followed the same pattern as Jewish immigration to the United States (see Taylor

1971, 51–65). Immigration statistics are not available for Gypsies as a separate nationality. Many who might otherwise have been understood to be Gypsies described themselves as Russians, Poles, Hungarians, or Serbians, either choosing to cite their nationality rather than a specific ethnicity or actually understanding themselves to be (and others seeing them as) Russian, Polish, and so on.

After the United States passed restrictive immigration legislation in 1924 (Taylor 1971, 253), Sway (1988) argues that eastern European Gypsies began immigrating to Mexico, Central America, and South America, and to a lesser extent to countries in the Caribbean basin. According to Hancock (1987), the difficulties posed in terms of entry to the United States caused many Gypsies to buy Argentinean documents and thus enter the United States as nationals of that country. He goes on to suggest that many Russian Gypsies sailed for South America and subsequently made their way overland along the Pacific coast into the United States. However, it is as problematic to establish that these people coming into the United States via South America were in fact Gypsies as it is to demonstrate that those groups and individuals labeled Gypsies who may have been transported or migrated to the New World in the colonial and immediate postcolonial period were in fact Gypsies.

For Hancock, this alternative immigration strategy explains why so many Gypsies living in the United States today speak Spanish and have ties to various Latin American countries. It may also be the case that their language and connections evidence nothing more than a South American origin.

If the above is placed alongside Hancock's contention that "many Gypsies . . . have learned to melt more effectively into the larger society and that Gypsies themselves will frequently deny their identity," who then is determining this identity? If the Gypsies have melted into the larger society or deny Gypsy identity, it can't be an identity made by Gypsies. By his own analysis, Hancock seems to be indicating that in the American context Gypsy identity is the construct of theorists, writers, or others with political interest in defining an American Gypsy lineage. As such, the category in the American context seems vulnerable, or even not viable.

The Lost Gypsy

For Hancock:

> *Non-Gypsy populations receive most of their knowledge of Gypsies from works of fiction and from the media, rather than from Gypsies themselves. Journalists and novelists for years have had completely free reign to exploit their fantasies in print, comfortable in the knowledge that no one would be likely to challenge them—and certainly that no Gypsy ever would. A traditional, fictional image of the Gypsy, of non-Gypsy origin, has emerged and has become so deeply entrenched in the popular mind that the real thing remains unseen.*

It seems much of the literature surrounding American Gypsies falls into this trap.

According to Hancock:

> *"Real" Gypsies no longer exist; they are a part of a vanished folk culture. . . . Books and articles have been written which refer to Gypsies as "hidden" or "invisible" Americans, and Gypsies make good use of this fictional image as a shield between themselves and outside society, even giving it back if it is in their interests to do so.*

He agrees with Okely that "Outsiders have projected onto Gypsies their own repressed fantasies and longings for disorder" (1983, 232). For Hancock (1987), the historical catalog of anti-Gypsy laws in the United States has caused American Gypsies to hide their identity in order to avoid discrimination, and, since the end of World War II in particular, as Gropper (1975) has argued, the American Romany population has become increasingly urban and settled, though living invisibly to be free of harassment. For Hancock, this gradual integration has led to assimilation and the loss of traditional language, culture, and identity. This being the case, alongside other considerations highlighted in this chapter and this book, the idea that there can be a discernible Gypsy ethnic or racial viability in the American context seems unrealistic. The overall analysis of the Gypsy presence in the United States, if it ever existed as an appreciable or significant phenomenon, argues that the category, alongside its cultural artifacts, has disappeared due to social and biological factors. This leaves a strange argument:

1. There was a Gypsy presence in America.
2. This presence has dissipated.
3. There is (a largely invisible) Gypsy presence in America.

This is more serious than a contradictory analysis; it is not so much a mirage as it is sleight of hand.

Conclusion

This chapter has analyzed the historical background from which the American Gypsy population emerges. I suggest that those groups that much of the literature sees as the progenitors of the current Gypsy population, the transported during the colonial era and subsequent immigrants categorized as Gypsies, may not have, in reality, been ethnically, racially, or even socially Gypsies. I conclude by asserting that this analysis, together with the contemporary notion that current American Gypsies are so absorbed into the greater host population that they deny their own existence and become invisible, brings the whole notion of an American Gypsy into doubt.

5

Gypsies in Social Bondage

As pointed out in chapters 2 and 3, the literature concerned with Gypsy identity does not address the overarching factors that pull the Gypsy category together. In fact, there seems to be agreement that Gypsies are united by their difference: groups or even particular families are the same because they are different from each other. This proposal is inherently contradictory. The reverse logic would be to claim that identical entities are distinctive from each other because they are indistinguishable. Each position is clearly nonsensical, having lost claim of logic and rationality. As such, in this chapter I demonstrate that there is little to suggest that Gypsies can be seen as an ethnic, racial, biological, or historical whole. I will look at the means by which Gypsies are socially agglomerated. It is my contention that the diversity of people that might be labeled as Gypsies are subject to certain social structural bonding agents that continually generate and maintain the category.

Gypsy Affiliation and Law: Playing Cards with Darkie

> *What I am is already decided before I open my mouth. Who or what I am is how I live. The law keeps us all in our neat little holes. That's how it deals with us.* (Darkie Charles, Alabama)

I have often looked at the above statement and wondered if that is how social categorization actually works. I played cards with Darkie during a time I lodged in one of his trailers while in his employ picking apples. While what I like to think was my skill (but probably had more to do with my luck) at poker supplemented my meager wage (Darkie insisted I had laid a hex on him), he told me how he was a Gypsy.

> *I have never been to no school. My whole life I've not been in the employment of no one. I never paid a cent in tax, and no insurance man has had a penny from me.*

For all this, as far as I could tell, Darkie was a wealthy man. He paid people, mainly illegal immigrants, to pick fruit, although according to Darkie his work force was "Gypsies like you and me" (this was followed by a deep belly laugh). "A grower pays me to get his fruit picked, I get it done." The only legitimate American Darkie seemed to associate with was Max, a man with a dark, pockmarked face who chauffeured him around in a big, ancient snow white Buick (Darkie had never bothered to acquire a license). Max was retired and spoke in a thick Mexican accent; he was the third member of our card school. He told me,

> *Some of Darkie's payment for getting the fruit picked he gets in fruit. He sell it to shops, or he pay people to sell it on the roadside. He done that all his life. None of it legal. He dodged the law all his life. His daddy was the same. Maybe his daddy's daddy too.*

Darkie was well aware that he existed as a social anomaly:

> *The law says that people like me are "something," and that makes us that something.*

Here he made it clear that he understood that he was notionally and in practice defined by law, as much as he avoided the means of that definition; he knew that the very fact that he lived, to a great extent, outside social controls actually defined him as a legal category. He was also quite good at helping others become more aware of how the law can define them:

But you's outside the law yourself son, else you wouldn't be working for me, and you wouldn't be taking my money. Maybe I should report you (he laughed).

Over the years I have thought and written about Gypsy identity, the ring of insight in Darkie's observations has grown ever more apparent. Hancock (1987) argues that methods of law enforcement have created degrees of unity among Gypsies that grow from a common feeling of oppression and experience of injustice. Historically, modern methods of control can be seen to be no more than recent variations on a traditional theme:

When, over the centuries, this tactic of expulsion proved limited or ineffective, the only alternative was to confine the dissidents: in prisons, in factories, or under daily police surveillance on the fringes of society. (Liegeois 1986, 104)

Liegeois argues that Gypsies have been a constant target for persecution, and, although he fails to consider the fact that any legislation affecting itinerant groups or those living outside social norms has an impact on Gypsies and non-Gypsies alike, what becomes clear from his analysis is that

1. many groups of people have been categorized as Gypsies,
2. these groups are categorized as Gypsies because of their unconventional or transient ways of life, and
3. this unconventional or transient way of life is the basis of persecution rather than Gypsyness.

The above would certainly apply to Darkie Charles, but also to others I have cited in this book who themselves represent my lifetime experience of so-called Gypsy culture.

Categorization: A Space of Weak Power

Okely (1983) is aware of the advantages of creating a homogenous Gypsy identity and that a racial or ethnic grouping can prove useful to groups that have no other means of combating oppression. As Stuart Hall has pointed out:

> *Paradoxically, marginality has become a powerful space. It is a space of weak power, but it is a space of power nonetheless.* (Hall 1991, 34)

For Hall, the weak and oppressed are placed at the margins of society and as such have no access to the conventional routes to power. This being the case, they make the source of their marginality an asset. Okely does not overtly state that this may be a primary force behind the manufacture of an analysis that suggests that Gypsies have common origins, but she does state that

> *Traveler groups are as much a social construction as a genetic or biological entity.* (1983, 35)

According to Okely, a Gypsy race does not exist (1983). But she goes on to note that the portrayal of Gypsies as a persecuted racial collective can provide the impetus for solidarity. However, this perspective may also be counterproductive. The taking on of the identity of the oppressed can become a means to gain resources: a sort of passive-aggressive response. Therefore, it is in the interest of the self-proclaimed oppressed to continually assert (preserve) their oppressed (deficit) status. Certainly, Darkie invested in this perspective:

> *I let people know why they don't like me. It pays to be honest* (he chuckled).
> *They tell me "You're a Gypsy," and I tell 'em that's the reason why they come chasing me more than say murders or child molesters. That it's because I'm a Gypsy and employing Gypsies* (Darkie laughed again). *They back off a little then. They don't like to be called no racist.*

Here, Darkie is embracing a social identity and, from his point of view, is using it against those who might not have his best interests at heart. The adoption of roles described by others is something warned against in the colonial context (Fanon 1967; Biko 1986); the process can be part of the wider control nexus—

"we are at a disadvantage (not as strong) as they; that is why we have an inferior status." However, this position allows the disadvantaged to accuse others (the advantaged) of bullying or oppressing them. This gains the moral high ground and what might be thought of as pseudopower, in that it is premised on making the advantaged feel responsible for the position of the disadvantaged. It is not authentic power, because the relative social positions (oppressed and oppressor/dominated and dominant) have not changed. In fact, the social roles are confirmed and ossified by such behavior in that the dominated group has not taken responsibility for itself but merely acknowledges that all responsibility for the social hierarchy lies in the hands of the dominant group. This is precisely the position that Fanon (1967) and Biko (1987) see as necessary for the perpetuation of colonial relations. This analysis highlights the possible political and social outcomes of ethnic categorization and the acceptance of the same.

Taking on, agreeing to, or adopting a collective Gypsy identity, as framed by professionals (including professional Gypsies), academics, politicians, born-again Romanies, or other interested parties, with more or less overt agendas, offers social benefits and power. It is equally transparent that this is a tepid authority, based on the accusation of wider guilt (the guilt of non-Gypsies), awarded by power elites to those ready to assume the bogus crown of the oppressed. However, to paraphrase Biko, the moment one takes on the identity of the oppressed, one is in fact oppressed. Freedom from oppression begins with the casting off the label of the oppressed. Darkie was quite clear about his position in relation to the rest of society:

> *There is nothing I can do about me. I am who and what I am. I learned how to live from my father, and he learned from his old man. I got nothing to do with the way society sees me. I can't do a thing about that. I was born at the bottom of the pile, and they would keep me there. I just don't let 'em push me around without telling 'em that's what they're doing. That way they leave me alone to just get on with being me.*

When I first entered the professional academic environment, I was taken as a straight white man. My supervisor (a kind of personal mentor found widely in the field of informal education and youth work) told me that this made me "the naffest creature possible" within the context of my work and that my "East London accent was associated with racism." I was advised to take elocution lessons, in effect to hide and apologize for my apparent identity. I was surrounded by others who by their association with oppression seemed to be in a better position than I; black, gay, and female colleagues had a resource while I, because of the way I looked and sounded, had guilt, being the seeming source of their relative authority. My working-class origins and what felt like innate political affinities, very much the product of the history of industrial struggle and social solidarity that the area of my birth was associated with, meant nothing.

My family had never encouraged me to talk about my Gypsy connections. Though not entirely a font of shame, the pronouncement of such affinities seemed inappropriate, probably because I had not been educated to see my identity as a weapon or a means of defense; it just was. For some time, although actively involved in issues and work connected with Gypsies, it did not even occur to me to use my background to make or win a point. But it was at a professional meeting where someone had begun a statement, "As a vegetarian, I'd just like to say. . . ." This was followed by others using similar predicates: "As a gay man," "As a person of color," "As other-able." Almost without a thought I found myself saying, "As a working-class Gypsy." I neither recall the point I was making, nor if I could have envisaged a middle- or even upper-class Gypsy at the time. I am pretty sure that no one listened to what I had to say after my first sentence. The collective look of the thirty or so people present was a cross between puzzlement and shock. At that time, in that place, to those people, I had said something akin to, "I am a thieving vagabond." Perhaps I should have used some euphemism, maybe Traveler or Romany; but the word I knew best as me was Gypsy.

Two things had happened here: I had succumbed to social pressures to admit to or use my identity, perhaps feeling bereft, vulnerable, or misunderstood otherwise, and in the process I had taken on the weak power identified by Hall (1991, 34). However, I think there had been a third force in operation; the motivation of my response was a subtle but collective discrimination arising out of a social propensity to categorize others according to assumptions based on limited, surface traits. But the very statement "I am one of them" starts the ball of affiliation rolling and it is not premised on political affinity, ideological beliefs, values, attitudes, or even forms of care. In that context, the principle of identity demarcation says little more than "I am different from you, and I am oppressed" and "You are not the same as me; you oppress me." It is a competition set in an arena of guilt and shame. But as Darkie Charles told me,

> *Flip the coin of guilt, and on the other side is resentment. Shame a man, and you get no thanks; all you get is his resentment for your trouble.*

This is weak power, but it may be all that is available to the Gypsy if access to conventional forms of political organization seem unachievable. Such a feeling might be the product of an amorphous category (Gypsies) that does not see itself, despite the insistence of academics and officials, as a homogenous whole. More precisely, the apparent lack of Gypsy political solidarity may betray the disparate nature of the Gypsy population. This, again, throws doubt on notions of shared identity or origin, the basis of organization perhaps being more a form of social categorization than some fundamental connection of ethnicity, blood, race, or shared origin.

Marketing Gypsies

Those who are active in promoting the Gypsy population as a definite collective may well be attracted by other motives. As Liegeois states:

> *The Gypsies, like many other minorities, are highly marketable these days. The fashion for Gypsies has now become a feature of the environment in which they live. This threat to turn their culture into spectacle is a danger more difficult to apprehend than the effects of the*

> *various regulations or of social work and schooling. There is now a risk that lack of respect will give way to pseudo-respect. In some ways this is worse, because it is garbed in an insincerity and fraternalism that are more dangerous than the paternalism that preceded it.*
> (Liegeois 1986, 180)

This might be understood as a critique of the romantic tradition found in the literature. However, at worst the general theme of the literature appertaining to Gypsies engenders aimless guilt; at best it constitutes a kind of marketing exercise wherein the Gypsy is presented as a constant victim. Liegeois is clearly identifying the motivation of some writing on Gypsy issues. The identification of the other, seen in a positive light, marks out uniqueness and difference that can easily be reinterpreted as strange or alien. In an academic and intellectual environment it is difficult to sustain a doctrine of innate human differentiation based on race (see Montagu 1968, 1975, 1997; Stepan 1982) that includes prescriptions that certain types belong in particular places. However, it is acceptable to take a position supporting ethnic diversity or distinctiveness and campaign for the rights of labeled individuals and groups to be placed in their own cultural space. It may not be that some writers on Gypsies have a conscious hidden racist agenda. However, as Liegeois recognizes, the desire for ethnic categorization might be stimulated by unconscious forms of class anxiety, discrimination, and prejudice. The potential for discriminatory motivation is especially disturbing when ethnic categories seem to be based on very insubstantial premises. But it is the insidious process of transforming socially motivated categorization into ostensible inherited biological differences that has the potential to be a very dangerous and destructive force, which was most painfully evident throughout the twentieth century. It is at this level, the macro level, that the subtle identification of ethnic types must be seen to be fully understood.

The Categorization Trap

The inherent problem with the entire campaign that works to formulate Gypsy collectivity as essentially a racial or ethnic collectivity is that it helps generate and confirm rights for and defense under the law of those adopting, inheriting, or being conscripted to Gypsy identity. This group is, as such, dependent on this single, highly questionable strand of commonality: the rights of and laws affecting Gypsies refer to an ethnic whole; and in order to access defense under the law or enact rights after the law has been applied to Gypsy behavior, one is obliged to identify oneself as a Gypsy. In law, if one acts like a Gypsy or is understood or portrayed to act how a Gypsy is supposed to act (undertaking activity that is outside social norms), then in order to claim a right or defend oneself in law one needs to identify oneself as a Gypsy (even if one is not of this ilk in terms of tradition, inheritance, etc.). Failure to do this results in defenselessness.

Ethnicity and Social Closure

In this section, I will continue to demonstrate how social forces and interaction give rise to ethnic categories and, in particular, will look at some of the channels through which Gypsy ethnicity has been generated and developed to produce a central binding agent of the group.

It has been argued that forms of social exclusion are important factors in the social generation of ethnic categories (Banton 1987, 199; Woodward 1997, 29, for example). Weber (1922, 147) also saw exclusionary forces as impacting the formation of ethnic affinities:

> *Ethnic membership does not constitute a group; it only facilitates group formation of any kind, particularly in the political sphere. On the other hand, it is primarily the political community, no matter how artificially organized, that inspires the belief in common ethnicity.* (1922, 389)

For Weber, social closure is a means by which certain social groupings monopolize particular resources. Access to these resources is reliant upon the possession of prescribed social or physical circumstances, be these of a negative or positive nature. Those to whom access is denied form a category (or categories) that is outside: they occupy an area of exclusion in terms of economic or social opportunities, relative to those who exist above the high-water mark of closure. This is clearly the case for Darkie Charles and others I have cited throughout this book, and it was obvious to Darkie:

> *I was never allowed in. I never will be. I do what I gotta. They got the inside, I got the outside. But that's my inside* (he smiled broadly).

According to Weber, the tactical character of exclusion and the permeability of social closure define the nature of the total system of distribution in any given society wherein stratification is the norm. Weber sees that in such societies the predominant form of closure is of the above nature.

Parkin (1979) refines and expands on Weber's theory and considers the deployment of closure strategies on the part of those who have been defined as ineligible, in order to resist the dominance of the excluders. The following narrative exemplifies this process in a personal, psychological perspective. It is taken from part of a conversation with Sparrow, a so-called New Age Traveler, someone not from a lineage of travel, but a person who has taken to an itinerant way of life in a response to his experience of social exclusion:

> *I had no way of identifying with the way of life I had before I took to the road. It was just that my life seemed to have nothing to do with me. As you learn to travel, or part of learning to travel, is adapting to environments. If you have to live on vegetables that's no big deal—you just do. Most people who don't travel couldn't do that, but it's that which seemed to be more me: the adaptation thing. We do not serve the clock. I don't even have a clock! That's difficult for people who don't travel. I'm not too interested in time. Day's for waking, night's for sleeping.*

Sparrow distinguishes himself from the norm. His self-identification, not being that of most people, and his feeling excluded from that grouping as a consequence, align him with a we that he portrays as and finds evidence for being different. This very difference excludes non-Travelers, those unable to do the adaptation thing.

> Why travel? Why not? People have always traveled. Most of human history has involved nomadism. It's a bridge with the people of the past. Life itself is a journey. We are all leaving and arriving. The Aborigines in Australia, the Indians in America. They are spiritually connected to movement and the earth. Our lives are like tales of travel. It's not where you're going that matters, it's the way you go. You don't ask where a stream or a river is going—you just connect with its flow. You need nothing to travel. That's good. What you need comes to you. It's amazing how if you just ask someone for something, they will often just give it to you. I asked a guy for some diesel the other day. "Sure," he said. I offered to do his horoscope, but he was a Christian or something. Everything you need is in the journey, see.

The story develops into saying something like "I am natural; those who are not like me are not natural." Sparrow is a kind of real insider, and the majority, perhaps unknowingly, are the outsiders.

> I never feel permanent. I never did. It was the forces of the universe that drew me to where I am. That "human gravity" has a pull on certain spirits. Maybe those who have been this way before. As soon as we've had enough, we just leave; it is easy for us to do that. Our souls are sort of joined in that. I've stayed in places for months though. I was in a squat for nearly a year a couple of years ago. But I was still a Traveler, traveling. With us sometimes it's just enough to know that you can just go. You move to the cycles and seasons of the earth. She becomes your identity. I'm not a job or where I live. I am what I feel. The family I am with are "The Good Intent." I tell people that, and that says a lot about who I am, more than if someone tells you that they work in Marks and Spencer or something. We sometimes go places because we know that we fulfill a need.

It is striking how the process of spiritual inclusion and exclusion is active in Sparrow's narrative. I have found this to be something of a constant in terms of my interaction with Travelers of all descriptions, from Gypsies to traveling salespeople. It is almost typical that throughout Sparrow emphasizes difference with an underlying claim that his inclusion is more natural (better) than the inclusivity that he feels excluded from. If one were being cynical it could be interpreted as a species of inverted snobbery or compensation.

> *You move for different purposes. For work, but social connections as well. To link up with other groups and families. Collectivity is our strength. We are part of a spiritual whole. We need to mingle, take lovers, partners to travel the road with you. Travel is a mellowing thing. Or maybe not—traveling just winds you up. We are the wind. We need to blow across the land. I've got two kids with other families, and they are so mellow compared to kids who don't travel. They go to schools, and they don't like it compared to the Traveling schools. They find kids who don't travel very aggressive and immature.*

As the narrative continues, the suggestion becomes more overt that the society Sparrow initially left—feeling not to be a part of it, excluded—is contorted, abnormal, and destructive. It seems to be the driving force of the main source of the spiritual inclusion he now feels part of, an ethic of naturalness, which seems to be a metaphor for health.

For Parkin, the process of inclusion and exclusion amounts to a response to power exercised in a downward direction from excluders by power projected upwards by the excluded in order to gain greater access to resources. In effect, this is an attempt by those abstracted, in terms of legalized rights to privilege, to erode the juridical structure within which the existing exclusion is enshrined. Sparrow is, like Darkie Charles, in essence an outsider, a dissenter, who by his exclusion of the excluders rejects and revolts against structures erected by the state. Again this seems to be an archetype across those involved in a traveling lifestyle:

> *You gotta be an outsider to live this life. You gotta have your own regulations. There are others just like me. It's in yer blood. You gotta get out there and sell, never in one place long enough to get caught. Get your piece of the cake, and go! It's hard to hit a moving target. The highway's ma home. I ain't got no speed limits, and not drinking' 'n' drivin' is for settled folks. I'm a rambler and a gambler, and my pay*

packet tells me, "You ain't breakin' the fuckin' law, cause the fuckin' system ain't your system!" (Dick, traveling salesperson, Tennessee)

My dad told me, "You's always gonna be a traveling gal." He told me that, "there ain't no rules for Gypsies. Cause we's not part of no place." We makes our living outa our laws, no one but ours. You gotta take what you can get in this world. (Loretta, lifelong Traveler, Mississippi)

Parkin labels this disposition, when experienced within a wide social process, as usurpation (1979, 84–86). For him, social closure is the practice of exclusion that results in usurpation. Usurpation, as a mass phenomenon, may take the form of total expropriation, or at lower levels of action it can result in minimal changes in distribution. To whatever degree this is exercised, the process is equipped to confront structures of allocation and distribution. In terms of the generation of an ethnic identity, a justification for exclusion by the excluders can be founded on the premise of race or ethnicity, as in the colonial situation or the treatment of the Jews in Nazi Germany. Equally, the exclusion of the included by the excluded can be founded on racial or ethnic categorizations (for example, the Black Panthers, Rastafarians). The label of "Gypsy" has generated and provoked reference to the law (see Hancock 1987); this demonstrates how they as a group are legislated against (set apart and excluded in the law for being what they are). At the same time, the expressed wish on the part of Gypsies to be placed apart, as a distinct category, could be interpreted as a means to exclude the included.

Inclusion and Exploitation

Parkin sees that "exclusionary rules and institutions must always be justified by universal criteria that are indifferent to pretensions of stigmata or birth" (1979, 47). Parkin is arguing that any exclusionary regime must have a method of inclusion, based on legitimate forms of usurpation, that creates motivation on the part of the excluded to propagate the prevailing system (i.e., entry into the elite). This undermines the possible alignment of the excluded into movements aimed at total expropriation of the areas of privilege cornered by the excluders. For Parkin, the attainment of qualifications and the institutions of property constitute the apparatus of exclusion in capitalist society. According to him, it is these mechanisms that act as the gatekeepers to resources. As such, exclusion is at the heart of the social and legal structures of modern Western society. I have shown how Gypsy ethnicity (and by association ethnicity in general) can be an extraordinary form of qualification or property that can include the acquisition of weak forms of power. I have also demonstrated that ethnic or racial membership is not reliant on birth, but can be ascribed or adopted. Even when an individual inherits definite physical, ethnic traits such as color, this, in itself, does not disqualify movement through the exclusionary apparatus. Indeed, the physical identification of ethnicity can in itself be used (by both excluders and excluded) as a type of qualification. It is possible to argue that Gypsies are excluded (from non-Gypsy society) by economic, social, and legal considerations (see, for example, Hancock 1987). The pressure of law heightens the incidence of poverty, and this affects the potential of the labeled Gypsy for social inclusion by way of property. At present, an itinerant way of life restricts educational opportunities (Hawes and Perez 1995, 89) and health care (Hawes and Perez 1995, 109–12), thus limiting opportunities to gain qualifications. This demonstrates that ethnicity, of itself, does not necessarily prevent inclusion. The inability to gain access to social resources is at the hub of exclusion.

Parkin conceptualizes property in the Durkheimian manner, as the

> *right of a given individual to exclude other individuals and collective entities from usage of a given thing.* (Parkin 1979, 53)

but he sees property as capital, not as possession, as being "germane to the analysis of class systems," because property as capital "confers the right to deny access to the means of life and labour" (1979, 53). It is property as capital that gives legal power to an elite to limit accessibility to the means of production; property as capital embodies exclusionary rights that limit the life chances of those who are excluded. As the state gives rights (enforceable legal guarantees) to some, yet denies access to the means of life and labor to others, exploitation is part of the nature of the social closure/exclusion system. Ethnicity and race are bound up in the legal system through a huge field of legislation (see Hancock 1987 with regard to Gypsy ethnicity and the law). In respect to Gypsies, the legal power of an elite excludes them from access to the means of life and labor, including work, welfare, health provision, and housing. A Gypsy is not excluded and cannot, in law, be excluded from the same legal rights as a non-Gypsy because he or she is a Gypsy. However, Gypsies are excluded because their access to the means of life and labor is limited via their social position. This obliges many to either adopt the kind of position Darkie Charles has developed or to merely melt into the whole.

The Nature of Exclusion

Given that we exist in an exploitative environment, the excluded may seek to usurp power and resources from above to gain inclusion. They may gain inclusion via legitimate usurpation, attaining a legitimate share in the exclusionary regime. For example, Gypsies can and do gain inclusion via property (Darkie Charles) and/or taking on a way of life more consistent with broad social values. This will bolster the exclusionary regime as it complies with the norms and functions of that order. However, legitimate usurpation can, in theory, be taken to a maximum that would translate to expropriation. Why then is it that the outsiders—the excluded—do not aspire to this maximum potential?

Portrayed within Parkin's work there are two dimensions of the nature of contemporary social closure that may go some way in answering this question. First, he suggests that the excluding element is in a state of constant flux. Second, and out of this, he implies exclusionary tactics in contemporary society place emphasis on the individual (although social closure is applied both on individuated and collective levels). So, for example, Gypsies can be recruited into positions of influence within institutions and agencies that complement and confirm the exclusionary regime (Gypsies like me!). For example, they can become community leaders or executives of organizations concerned with the promotion of Gypsy rights and interests (professional Gypsies).

Parkin (1979, 61) concludes that the requirement of conformity often takes precedence over birth in terms of inclusion via credentials. It is lack of conformity, in terms of a range of social norms, that is the primary aspect that situates Gypsies within the ranks of the excluded (à la Sparrow and Darkie Charles). Parkin sees that adherence to doctrine is more fundamental to achievement than kinship with regard to entry into the ranks of the included; he aligns this condition with George Orwell's feelings about the communist party oligarchies, wherein he perceives that a "persistence of a certain world view" is critical and that concern lies with "the Party . . . perpetuating itself, not its blood" (1979, 63). Bourgeois values persist, not family lineage. As such, the rationale of the social order constructs and reinforces a system of exclusion and inclusion. The personnel of the elite are, to a large extent, in a state of liquefaction from generation to generation and also between generations. This argument shows that ethnicity is not central to considerations of inclusion. What is crucial is the regard of social norms. So, for those deemed as Gypsies and those ordained to be Gypsies, the rejection of the discipline of social expectations is what might be called the categorical imperative. Again, this is clear in the narratives I have presented in this book.

Individuated Social Closure

Although Parkin concludes that patterns of exclusion do not conform to any one typology and that social closure tends both to be referred to collectivities and be individuated, he sees a contemporary movement toward a more individualist form of exclusion, as the excluded become less identifiable within the total social context both by other outsiders and by excluders. This situation, according to Parkin, has tended to negate the fertile ground of "movements and ideologies" which raised questions about the nature of the political order and its legitimacy, and not merely about the fact of equal shares" (1979, 68). This orientation toward the individual would be consistent with the need Foucault (1977) recognizes for individuation in order to promote social control. The grouping together of excluded individuals, some of whom might carry the label "Gypsy," can be seen as a symptom of social closure and a form of legitimization. This being the case, Barth (1970) can be vindicated when he asserts that "the ascriptive aspect is logically prior to any objective characteristics of the ethnic group" (quoted by Guy 1975, 222). The social context can thus be understood to generate Gypsy identity, and that social closure is a generator of ethnicity.

Conclusion

The erection of a sameness-through-difference construct places Gypsies within an apparently fixed identity. This categorical chamber situates Gypsies within the parameters of an ethnicity that most writers concerned with Gypsies take part in creating, using a covert biological corral alongside behavioral and attitudinal considerations and claims about Gypsy tradition (see, for example, Acton 1974, 15–21; and, more explicitly, Kenrick and Bakewell 1990, 9–17). This essentialist position draws the reader toward notions of blood and race. In the case of Gypsies, unlike other enterprises of this type, it is not premised on the physical makeup of the body, but is seen to emanate from where the body is situated—that is, no fixed location and nonconformity to social norms. While providing some ground for solidarity, this essentialism is a powerful force that prevents any authentic political affiliation but produces an identity politics founded on being a Gypsy. Thus, the defining process proceeds as below:

1. Gypsies are ethnically (culturally, racially) distinct.
2. This is evidenced by their location and/or behavior.
3. The grounding of social solidarity is cultural (ethnically derived—nothing other).

4. Rights for and laws affecting Gypsies are framed in terms of ethnicity.
5. Access to justice, following the force of law being applied to Gypsy behavior (behavior that contravenes social norms), is maximized by the adoption of or ascription to an ethnic type.

This can provide only weak power, in that it delivers influence through the definition of self and others as different and oppressed, a classification that can at any moment be all too easily converted to alien and deficient by unsympathetic power elites (Montagu, 1968, 1975, 1997).

This process is but one way ethnicity is socially constructed; another is the process of social closure (Parkin 1979; Weber 1922). The distribution of social resources can be seen to contribute to the generation and maintenance of ethnic identity.

In the next chapter, I will show how this growth of ethnicity is further energized, confirmed, and complemented by narrative forces, which work to form a story of ethnic identity as a means of mundane explanation for the categorization of human beings into particular, distinct ethnic groupings.

6

Ethnicity as Narrative

In previous chapters, I have demonstrated that ethnicity is something defined socially—that is by the self—and how the self is defined by other selves. This chapter examines this proposition more closely by looking at the nature of the self and how the self and other selves develop the perception of ethnicity. From this basis I will argue that narrative is used as a means to generate and articulate Gypsy ethnicity. As such, the analysis includes an exploration of the role of narrative (see Bruner 1987; De Man 1984; Scheibe 1986) and social interactionist theory as pioneered by G. H. Mead (1934a; see also Hewitt 1979; Sutton-Smith 1986) in the development of Gypsy ethnicity.

Narratives as Meaning-Making Tools

As I grew up, my family went through several lines of business, most of them successful. My father had always been intent on somehow making it, breaking through the limitations he was born into. He saw money as his only real bridge to another life, and, for him, obtaining money was only (this was, for my dad, a law of life) possible through nefarious means.

As a child born at the start of the Depression years, my dad had been apprenticed into door-to-door selling, an occupation that was second nature to my grandmother. She would take him with her round the streets and from his pram he would proffer a bar of soap as prospective customers answered his mother's knock. It is much harder to refuse a baby than an adult. If you wanted a penny, you had to go and get a penny. That was the way of my family, and I initiated into this at a younger age, selling firewood from a barrow I pushed around my part of the East End of London.

Dad was, as such, a born trader. However, nothing ever seemed to be good enough; things always seemed to move too slowly, and gradually he lost hope. The demise of his golden if vague dreams caused him to search the barren fields of gambling and drugs in a frantic effort to find a way out. This led to the demise of venture after venture, despite his own hard work and the efforts of his parents, my mother, and, from five years of age, me.

Throughout my school life, my evenings and weekends were, in the main, taken up with two things: working in my father's timber business and following West Ham United, the most powerful of the cockney football teams, whose home field was a five-minute walk from where I was born. This relationship took me all over Britain and eventually to Europe and was the reason for my first visit to the United States.

Every November 5—Guy Fawkes/Bonfire night—we were obliged to fire-watch the family timber yard until the small hours of the morning. One such vigil I spent with my grandfather, as a myriad of fireworks cracked and soared while a million homemade pyres lit up the darkly mad, utterly winter East End sky. My father's father, staring into our own little brazier that created a warm but tight circle of gold for us, made what has always felt like a confession to me about his time spent in Norway during the war:

> *I took six Germans prisoner. I was on my own. I didn't know what to do with them. After a while, one of them approached me. "You want a cigarette Tommy?" he said, holding out a packet of fags. I had a tommy-gun. I shot the lot of 'em dead. It was terrible.*

My grandfather's education had concluded at the age of twelve. He was, as we would say, "out of the old town." This title marked a person from Canning Town, the area of the West Ham borough that produced some of the hardest men to inhabit the hard easterly extremities of the capital of the British empire. "The Town" at that time was barely more than a slum region: a sprawl of industrial nightmare dotted with swiftly built workers' cottages with no baths and, at best, one outside privy per house.

My granddad had worked most of his life as a stoker in the gas works. This was hellish employment, situated deep underground. Stokers worked naked apart from the steel boots they wore to protect them from the burning ground they stood on. Each man consumed a gallon of salted water per shift to replace the fluids and minerals lost in their labor. Jim Belton was an urban barbarian, obliged, during the years of the Depression, to fight bare-knuckle on the cobbles of the docklands for the right to house his wife and young child; only the deadly filterless "Woodbines" that hung continuously from his lips, that were to eat away his bowels before he reached his mid-sixties, could stop him. But that night, the flames that protected us from the biting cold glinted in his watery eyes:

> *I had never been anywhere before. Never out of England. We went to Norway by ship. We got to what they called the fiords. . . . The sea was like a silver cloud. . . . It was like we were floating on mercury. . . . We were all saying, "What the fucking 'ell is this?" A sailor told me . . . "Them's sardines." It was unbelievable! Fucking Sardines!*

The only place my granddad had seen sardines was in a tin.

This story tells me quite a lot about myself, who I am, my influences. The reader is also told a great deal in a mere eight hundred words. Reading this tale, among other things, you see something of what the East End of London was and is like, and you gain insight into the liberation of a country and a continent and maybe into the nature of war. But you also see snapshots of individual psyches—my father's and my grandfather's—and my own disposition. There is no mention of Gypsies or ethnicity, although the theme of identity runs throughout the narrative.

Narratives might be understood as meaning-making tools. They shape our view of the world. We adopt narratives in an effort to make sense of the complexities of life and are, as such, constantly using them to construct meaning: Who are the people in front of me? What motivations and restrictions do they have? And so on. One short visit to a Gypsy site (a housing estate or a project) might provide ample evidence for the storied nature of life; in such places, stories collide, coalesce, and develop. We bring our stories together, and these stories shape the collective meaning. That meaning emerges as a narrative, but is later reformed into reports, descriptions, case studies, and so on. As exemplified in the story of my grandfather, human experience is storied, and the meaning-making process of the storyteller (the researcher or reporter) is also storied. The story is a net in which we try to capture experience. This gives narratives an almost sacred role; our sense of self and wider existence is made by these stories. Stories about ourselves and the world exist within the stories and are the building blocks of consciousness.

The storyteller tells others about his or her life in a way that can be understood, which is the great appeal of stories; we can relate to them because they are about an example of us (humanity). The story of my granddad tells me about me. Like my dad, I am a dissatisfied man; there seems to be more to this world than what there is for me (and it is also the story of all dissatisfied people). Did I get this from him or from the stories of him? Certainly, living with him and the tutelage of my grandmother, a woman who never stopped wanting, seem to have had their effects on me. I am tempted, at times, because of the seeming restlessness of my soul, to adopt the same kind of genetic, biological standpoint of most writers on Gypsy issues. "Traveling is in my blood" feels like an easy way out of my psychic quandary and an excuse not to question it; if it is in me, what can I do about it? But this, and maybe the entire enterprise of genetic excuse making through wish-fulfilling science, says more about the force of narrative than anything else.

The narrative is above all an interpretation. Interpretation is an effort to find meaning. Understanding always comes before interpretation, and without it there is no interpretation.

I have always understood myself to be an East End Gypsy; however, over the last quarter of a century I have tried to interpret what this means. It has led me to study other interpretations of this identity. My Gypsy life in the United States of the mid-1970s was perhaps the start of this process. I was told that the way I lived was typically Gypsy but also that I was not a Gypsy at all. Each of these assertions or interpretations was justified with life stories or narratives that exemplified my Gypsiness or otherwise. "A Gypsy wouldn't do the work you do. We do creative work. We work for ourselves, not other men." "Like all Gypsies, you know how to gamble. My father wouldn't lay a dime on a dog unless he knew it was going to win, and he was always right." The interpretations are apparently unending, but things start with an understanding, although that understanding might change in the light of interpretation.

So the telling of a story of one's life or experience is a shared exploration of the meaning of events and an attempt to make things clear. So narratives are not merely some sort of reproduction of reality, like a photograph. They are interpretations that allow us to engage in interpretation and comprehend the world in ways that are novel to us and help us to communicate new ideas to others. The stories of others provide us with a means to develop meaning as we assimilate experiences into our own narrative of self. This makes narrative a ubiquitous and powerful tool in the construction of identity.

The Self, the I, and the Me

Together with social exclusion, Woodward (1997, 29) suggests that forms of symbolic representation also play a part in the social construction of ethnic categories. The symbolic interactionist's view of the self is a perspective that places the construction of the self within a framework of a process. This process involves a development of the concept of the generalized other, which the individual constructs, through particular confrontations, to form a guide to his or her actions (see Strauss 1964, xxiii–xxiv; and Hewitt 1979, 45–65). The view of the self put forward by the symbolic interactionist is that the self is a social product; each self is representative of the group that is the generalized other. However, the individual is also more than this. This must be so, since people do not always conform to the uniform code that would be the behavior of the interpreted generalized other. The individual has the capacity to inculcate his- or herself into the overall pattern of existence. The ability to reflect on one's own actions creates a process of development of the self, wherein the outside world feeds expectations into the individual. The individual interprets these expectations and acts on them. At the same time, the individual exchanges this transmission with a transmission of his or her own, and thus he or she has a part in the generalized other that other individuals receive and act on. In this model, the Gypsy is defined by the self and all other selves. As such, Gypsy identity is a product of social mutuality and is not some biological given. Derby, who told me he was from Irish Tinker stock and was therefore an honorary Gypsy, told me:

> *When I lived in New Orleans, everybody took me as Cajun. I look and act that way. I like the music, I like the food. I like that way of life. But here* (Orlando) *they say I'm Irish. Well, that's what I guess I am. But I don't go round saying, "Hey, I'm Irish." Like I never went round saying I'm Cajun. I just hang out with Irish type people the way I used to hang out with Cajun type people. It's the way I am, and people see that. So I guess I'm both Cajun and Irish. That's what it takes to be American, maybe?*

It can be seen that these interchanging expressions of transmission and reception shape the self, but the self is its own architect as well as a contributor to the self of others. This construction that is manufactured from both the collective and the unique has its dynamic in the work of George Herbert Mead (1934a, 1934b) on the I and me. For Mead, the I and the me form a dialectic within the self, the me constantly reflecting on the actions of the I, which are the direct responses to objects in the environment. As such, the I dictates to the me, while the me shapes the I.

In terms of the construction of Gypsy ethnicity, this process might be seen to operate as follows:

1. The me, who exists as a Gypsy, reflects on the actions of this I.

2. The actions of this I are responses to objects in the environment and the interpretations and subsequent actions taken by others that, for example, define the I as a Gypsy.
3. This is relayed to the me that in response shapes the Gypsy I.

The I and the me are not separated entities; in many ways, the division of the self into these two aspects is problematic. They are realms of consciousness that are considered separately only for the purposes of analysis. However, when the self is considered in this way one is better able to see that the self is more than the sum of the reaction to the expectations of other selves. The self can be understood to be a social expression, created by a unique conversation within the individual. The I gives out direct actions that are the result of its subjectivity. At the same time, the me is organizing attitudes toward the experiencing I, defining the self and how others see the self. In essence, this process is one of cooperation that creates in each of us components that are unique and others that are common. As such, identity can be understood to be a product of the I-and-me discourse. Gypsy identity is thus more than a given, arising out of blood, tradition, or culture; it is the result of collusion between psychological and social phenomena, being independent of these mental or communal factors in isolation but dependent on their interaction.

This situation is ensured both by the impulsive, spontaneous actions of the I and the fact that the me can at times make inaccurate interpretations and construct inappropriate conduct for the I. The generalized other can also feed the me information and expectations that conflict with existing models of the self that, in turn, influence the actions of the I. The I may then embark on what may deviate from the norm. Thus, it can be seen that the individual takes on the role of others responding to the self, and these roles are played on the basis of acquired knowledge about possible responses to actions undertaken. However, any response will be imbued with elements that are unpredictable and will produce from time to time something that is novel to the environment. This perspective negates the idea of a set Gypsy ethnicity as proposed in much of the literature relating to Gypsy identity in that novel forms of behavior can arise. However, because the Gypsy role will be played according to what are seen as possible responses of Gypsies, it also means that the prevailing understanding of Gypsy identity will be preserved.

The construction of narrative, insofar as it is a projection of the self, can be seen as a product of symbolic interaction. As a reflective presentation and an object, it requires both states of consciousness residing in the self to be deployed. It is also received, interpreted, and acted upon, and in this process becomes a material interaction. Narrative contains expressions that could be seen as imparted by the generalized other and expressions that are novel ideas and have unique meanings (see Sutton-Smith 1986). If only narrative existed (so even the presentation of the self would be no more than a narrative), what would be the genesis of the narrative? The following will explore the theory that the self is prior to the narrative of it, that the self exists, albeit expressed in a narrative form. It will go on to propose that Gypsy ethnicity is a narrative and that something, a human being, exists prior to the label of "Gypsy" that is applied through narrative. Within this, it is understood that we may not see the self unmediated and that each renarration of the self takes us further away from that self (the more we elaborate on the narrative about Gypsies the further we get from the person), but it places the self at the starting point of the narrative rather than, as is the case in much of the literature relating to Gypsies, beginning with the product of the narrative, the Gypsy. I will also discuss the location of the self within descriptions of the narrative and show that it is necessary to the social formation.

The Narrative as an Expression of the Self: The Self Asserting Its Existence

According to Stuart Hall:

> *Histories have their real, material, and symbolic effects. The past continues to speak to us. But it no longer addresses us as a simple, fac-*

> tual "past," since our relation to it, like the child's relation to the mother, is always-already "after the break." (Hall 1994, 395)

For Hall, the break is made by the history of colonialism. He argues that knowledge was interpreted through colonialist domination that caused those who were dominated to see themselves as the other. What Hall is suggesting is that history is not what was but a version of what was, which is shaped by the social environment and subjectivity. As such, it has two levels of explanatory power. It tells us a version of what was and something about the type of society that shaped the understanding of what was. This being the case, our knowledge of the past is not an untarnished reflection of what was. It is a way of telling something given the confines of a given social milieu. It is a narrative construction.

Sutton-Smith suggests that narrative has its source in play scaffolding (1986, 71): the play interaction between nurturers and children. The child imitates the adult transmission of play sequences (which signifies reception and at the same time is a countertransmission); but at a later stage of development the child begins to bring novel features into the games that were before played via imitation. Conformity and novelty are carried over into storytelling, wherein children display constant factors and similar patterns but also aspects of variation. Though the organization of narrative takes place around certain central actions or words, within this there are huge variations; this variation is added to by differences in pitch, tempo, beat, rhythm, rhyme, and placement of crescendos.

This perspective of the evolution of the narrative contains within it traces of the symbolic interactionists' view of the self—the me organizing the I with reference to the social environment and the I displaying novel action, operating directly on the object. Sutton-Smith (67–90) points out that to stage a story one must have an idea of oneself as a storyteller and of being in that role with an audience. This implies a sense of oneself as an object and an ability to view oneself from the perspective of others. Sutton-Smith (69–73), who clearly built on the thoughts of Erving Goffman (1959, 28–83), also suggests that there must be a conception of the story as a stage on which characters can be made to act in certain ways that mean that a repertoire of learned possible roles is called upon. Sutton-Smith's formulation of the formation of the storytelling act (in terms of its individual development) suggests that storytelling is reliant on the self and is the projection of it; insofar as the story is the precursor of the narrative it may be suggested that the narrative is an expression of the self. Gypsy ethnicity can thus be understood to be a narrative, a production of the self. My ethnic narrative is primarily an explanation of the way I live; it gives my life a context. However, much of the literature concerned with Gypsy ethnicity reverses this position, arguing that the context of a Gypsy's life marks out his or her ethnicity. The way of life is the narrative stage on which ethnicity is played out. This puts the ephemeral before the material, the story before the storyteller.

T. R. Sarbin (1986, 3–21) sees the narrative as a joint, collective construction that is deployed in order to make sense of seemingly unconnected events in the individual's life. For Sarbin, the role of the analyst is to help the individual create from an inconsistent or contradictory narrative a more ordered, rational, logical, or satisfying product. The ethnic narrative of the Gypsy might be understood to provide a similar conclusion, bringing heterogeneous elements into a homogenous whole. These imaginative formulations are able to meet tests of coherence (12). For Sarbin, we are able to make sense of our lives through the use of narratives; indeed, stories (the terms "narrative" and "story" are for Sarbin's purposes interchangeable) of all kinds are our means of making sense of our own roles and all possible roles. Sarbin also sees the narrative acting as a form of self-deception, in order to preserve or enhance the self-identity of the narrator. We are, in effect, seen as using stories to project a desired image into the social milieu. These constructs are only relative to the desired image and require minimal connection with reality in the first instance; however, as we construct these lives, we are, according to Sarbin, inclined to try to live them. Hence, Gypsy ethnicity becomes more and more real as the Gypsy works to construct his or her reality. In terms of Gypsy identity, the academic writing and inventing of Gypsy ethnicity can be seen as the counterpart to Sarbin's analyst in the construction of consciousness.

The self-narrative has relevance for Sarbin in the understanding of human actions in that he sees human beings as constructing identities through the imagination, via a range of stories, tales, and narratives. The life story of a person is a striving to live out this formulation. For Sarbin, the I is the author and the me is the actor, the narrative figure (18). The power of the self-author is to be able to create a future in the imagination and a reconstruction of the past. The narrative for Sarbin is a tool to facilitate understanding of the individual and as such can be beneficial in the therapeutic process. In terms of the construction of a Gypsy ethnicity we can see the past, Indian origins, and so on, as exemplifying a reconstruction of the past.

Sarbin suggests that the production of the self, which is produced with reference to, or the assistance of, the analyst and/or other narratives, does not undermine the conclusion that the self has an existence prior to the narrative. That the construction of the self-narrative might cause the individual to use this as an aim in life illustrates that the self is at least present; that it created or used the narrative, the fulfillment of which it seeks, gives it a first-cause status. Indeed, that we understand our lives via narratives implies that they are a language of the self. That we use this vocabulary to protect ourselves further punctuates the contention that the self exists prior to the narrative (just as language implies that thought exists beyond words, even if the words at a stage or stages shape thoughts) and that the narrative is an expression of the self. This is again reversed in formations of Gypsy identity wherein the identity of the Gypsy (the narrative) is seen to exist prior to the person (the self). Sarbin believes that the I and the me create narratives, however inaccurate they may be, and that they can be used as a pathway to the understanding of human actions (perhaps we can say the self); it would seem that for Sarbin the self has an independent existence (18). Therefore, the self is not Gypsy ethnicity; Gypsy ethnicity (as a narrative) is a product of the self.

Bruner (1987, 11–32) takes the constructionist view that sees the mind as involved in a world-making project; autobiography is seen as life making. Narratives are constructed in the mind and as such have only a tenuous link to the outside world. This said, the autobiography can only be an interpretation of our experiences, which is open to constant reinterpretation. Existence is molded and remolded in the mind; our exterior existence is but the material out of which our mind manufactures the product, the life. This being the case, the individual claiming or defining him or herself as a Gypsy is no more than the projection of a narrative; it is not a fact or the truth.

Bruner suggests that our only access to lived time is through the narrative; but as the construction, which is projected life, is intermediated by the interpretation process of the mind and the imagination, there can be no portrayal of the real existence. It is impossible to pass from the experience to its illustration; the distortion of interpretation cannot be avoided, an interpretation that is also reliant on the selective memory, the idiosyncratic ability to recall, which adds to the unreliability of any report of an event. Bruner deploys De Man's (1984, 84) thinking relating to the creation of the monument and the defacement that are implicit as the individual creates a commentary on him- or herself. These are similar to Sarbin's self-deceptive processes (Sarbin 1986, 16–17). The person cannot be detached from his or her life story; he or she may portray him- or herself as excessively evil or as uniquely angelic, but neither can be objective or real, because all is subjective and fabricated. Likewise, that which is related as intentional may have been accidental, a random event or an unintended consequence of some unintentional, random, or accidental happening. Bruner sees this reflexivity (1987, 13) of the self-narrative creating problems that bring the whole value of the construction into question. Added to all this are cultural, interpersonal, and linguistic influences that give a dynamic to the life story that creates an instability or substance. As such, one can see that self-ascription as a marker of Gypsy ethnicity is both stable and fragile.

For Bruner, cognitive and linguistic processes that are culturally defined shape experience and impinge on the institutions of the mind to such an extent that they create the life story (1987, 14). In the last analysis, we represent our culture; in turn, these accounts (1987) structure our life like Sarbin's (1986) self-constructions, via our own narratives—indeed, we become the accounts. But the person or the self is at the root of the Gypsy narrative; even if, over time, the self adopts this Gypsy identity, it can be understood that this is essentially a social construction. Gypsy identity is not necessarily the product of ethnic, hereditary, or blood factors. It arises out of mutuality between the individual self and other individual selves as a cooperative production. This argument sees the mind as creating the self-narrative, the projected self. This self-narrative and the self-narratives of others that one comes into contact with, however recounted, in turn shape the individual self. While Bruner seems to be undermining the self in asserting that the narrative creates the self and that the mind distorts reality in a way that makes inaccessible that which is real, he is, by making the mind the author of the self-narrative, illustrating that there is an aspect of the self that is prior to the narrative.

Bruner's version of the mind could be seen as containing the I and me constructs of the symbolic interactionists. The I (that is expressed in the world through the existing self-narrative) acts on the world. The me (the mind) organizes the attitudes one has to the same; the action involves commentating on the self (with reference to the generalized other), and the new self-narrative is emitted. As such, it is possible to become a Gypsy. The I comes into contact with other projected selves (other Gypsy narratives) and the me includes these in the self-definition. So, although the narrative is the language of the self and other narratives are used to add to this and elaborate the entire construct, the self can still be seen as being prior; I am myself before I am my ethnicity. But if Bruner is arguing that the self-narrative creates the self, that the mind (not being the self) distorts the reality so that which is real becomes totally lost, having no relevance to that which is the narrative, this sets up a Schopenhauerian problem (1818; see Flew 2002).

We, for all intents and purposes, cannot detect reality, because the equipment through which we view the world is restricted by its very makeup; we can only know that which we are allowed to know given our social formation, and that which there is beyond this is inaccessible. Therefore, we form a world of understandings that we comprehend through our limited senses, although this might have no relation to what it actually is. This said, it would seem that we are obliged to strive to connect with what we have as our reality, to refine reality as much as possible, and to seek to reach the nearest point we can to the truth. At the same time we need to understand our limitations, or we can simply abandon any attempt at viewing our lives, knowing what we bring forth is fundamentally the product of our own interior processing: that which this interior takes to be the exterior, which may have little relation to the real universe.

The mind is constantly constructing and reconstructing our reality. The reality of Gypsyness is in fact a mind construction. Gypsy ethnicity is a product of the personal and collective imagination or sentiment. It is born out of anxiety about the past and fear of the future. Crudely, it could be compared to a primitive belief or superstition. On the application of detached logic, it can be seen as an intangible, abstract, and contradictory construct. It seems that we can say that the event precedes the report of it, and if we say this we must surely also contend that the self is prior to the narrative. The narrative elaborates on reality; indeed it may go beyond the sensory equipment available; it may be right or wrong, but finding this out is the object of the operation of the total self (the I and the me). The self may only be available via the narrative, but from this we cannot make the leap to saying that all that exists is narrative. The very process of abstract thought seems to connote that there is more than the fulfilling of narratives in that thinking so often departs from previous narratives. Kuhn describes how this can be seen to work in scientific paradigms (in Crombie 1963, 347–69). He demonstrates how the process of scientific discovery often totally negates previous narratives. Bruner (1987) may be correct in feeling that any story could be better understood if other ways of telling it could be found, but can this mean a more accurate report? As such, the claim to Gypsy ethnicity means something; it cannot just be dismissed.

Spence explores the story-reality dilemma but concludes that whether one is elaborate in one's explorations, dwelling on incidents and refining what actually occurred, or if one uses quick sketchy reports, even free association, the reality cannot be reached. He addresses the problem in the psychoanalytic relationship and suggests that patient and analyst consort to deploy context and meaning to events and thus change historical truth (1982, 32, 292–97). This can be understood to be analogous to the construction of a narrative of Gypsy identity. The notion of an Indian diaspora for example can give meaning to an apparently meaningless situation. Spence sees the process of psychoanalysis as one of active construction of a patient's life story. The analyst creates order from the confused and distorted life events presented in the analytical context; this becomes the narrative truth and is implicit in the patient's cure. The theorists charting Gypsy ethnicity play a similar role. Like Bruner's (1987) idea of the mind as world maker, Spence sees this clinical relationship as a pattern-making plan (1982, 21, 33, 293), wherein order is created, not identified. For Spence, that which is past is converted into words and is re-created and transformed into something different than what existed before it was verbalized. In the same manner, Gypsy ethnicity is created at the expense of a more authentic understanding of the generation of the Gypsy population.

Spence argues that the self is a construction; the narrative constructed is the manifest form of the self. However, even this can be made redundant, as it is added to, detracted from, or remolded to adapt to any given change in the environment. Spence looks at the process that draws out our memories, thoughts, or dreams into verbalizations and the written word and the distorting influences on the original event. Thus we are compelled to convey these events via symbols that are inadequate to the accurate expression of the original events. Gypsy ethnicity is one or a collection of these symbols. It can be understood as a narrative construction of a tangible self, but it has the potential to be developed. This is the overriding aim of this book.

However, even if we had the mechanisms to convey our inner worlds accurately, temporal considerations would distort the view. Unless each aspect could be conveyed immediately, our emotions, insecurities, imagination, and processes of consideration would change the event; it would become an impression. We have and can have no access to the original event in the raw, but Spence sees the patient and analyst as creating a new event. Spence, given his own terms, implies that this event must itself disappear; but this is not what happens. Events are reorganized on the foundation of previously described events; these previously described happenings do not cease to be but, rather, are elaborated. As such, it is difficult to generate what might be thought of as a new paradigm of Gypsy identity, one that encompasses social and economic causation, as the foundation of Gypsy identity is made up of essentially ethnic, biologically determinist notions. In the construction of Gypsyness, personal and world histories are reinterpreted to give rise to an inherited Gypsy ethnicity.

Spence does not use Freud's metaphor of the analyst as archaeologist, because it seems unable to expose the problems brought to the analysis, due to the therapist's need to be aware of the archaeological metaphor as the basis of narrative and not its immediate forebear (1982, 263–78). But the materials out of which the narrative is wrought are the happenings of life; the archaeology is necessary to see the root of the narrative, even if this root can only be seen in the context of the narrative. The narrative is seen by Spence as an interactional creation between distinct selves. So, the construction of the narrative of Gypsy ethnicity needs to be understood as the product of mutuality, an agreement between definers and the defined. That the life narrative is not the life seems irrelevant (it would seem obvious), but the fact that the narrative is a construct in itself, in the last analysis, indicates a constructor or constructors, a self or selves (175). As such, historical facts or Okely's faith in social anthropological methods (1994, 1–3) as a door to authenticity are rendered no more than the raw material of interactive narratives.

That we cooperate to build the self-narrative, that we seek to elaborate our selves via role-taking and constantly forcing meaning from the actions of others and their reactions to our actions and then seek to integrate these reactions back into our own actions is confirmed by the view that we cooperatively construct life stories. That we cannot really show the self through which all this transpires seems relatively unimportant. What seems important is that we attempt to translate the self (via the narrative) and feel the need to form a view of the self for ourselves and others. This may be understood as the generator of Gypsy identity and all identity. Others seek to exhibit their selves to us, to enable them to know themselves better. It is this process of constant elaboration that gives us the ultimate clue into the existence of the self. That we use maybe the only available tool to interpret the self—the narrative—that at the same time plays a part in obscuring what we seek to lay bare—the self—is perhaps a necessary irony. However, it can only be through constantly elaborating on and questioning existing narratives that we move toward a more complete understanding of the meaning of, for example, the generation of Gypsy identity. As Bruner concludes via Yeats, "We may not be able to tell the dancer from the dance," but we can at least know that there are dancers and not just dances (1987, 32). There are people and not just ethnicities.

Scheibe (1986, 129–51) sees stories as a major source of human identity and argues that identity is a construction that is constantly evolving from an ongoing process of social interaction. For Scheibe, sport and gambling are examples of safe areas in which to use the vehicle of adventure to impart reasoned purpose into what was blind motive (1986, 131). The self is re-created via what Goffman (1959) called generation of character (Schiebe 1986, 135); what is produced is the self-narrative. The thrill (136) converts existing into living, positive self-construction. In short, this is the motive to move on from the formation of a Gypsy ethnicity that involves, at its base, the interpreting of various ethnic traits to the exposition of meaning—what do the generation and continuation of a Gypsy population reveal about the nature of our society and ourselves?

Scheibe excavates Guttman's work (1978) for quotations that exhibit this self-enhancement; "feeling that one exists," "discovering oneself," "finding an expression of the self," "knowing oneself" (Scheibe 1986, 136–37, 139) are expressions that exemplify the individual's striving to express that which is unique to them and the effort to know it. For Scheibe, this process is part of the construction of the self-narrative. Without adventure life becomes reduced to the tedium of conformity. We thus become stifled by replications of stereotypical depictions of Gypsy identity. Along with Bruner (1987) and Sarbin (1986), Scheibe argues that we retrospectively revise or select details of the past that give our present situations justification; we seek to create coherence and satisfaction. We thus build on what we have in terms of Gypsy identity. However, it would seem that Scheibe is identifying the I and the me—that is, the spontaneous and the reflective—creating the narrative. The self creates the narrative; the narrative is the expression of the self. Scheibe is describing the narrative in formation. He is showing that the self is explored in its elaboration. This is a search for meaning; although the narrative can be seen as adding to the self, the self is essentially at the core of the exercise, and the exercise is about not only substantiating, but also about exposing its true nature. I would argue that we have yet to confront the meaning or reality of our need to project an ethnicity, Gypsy or other, or the nature of the activity of the self and other selves in this process.

The Self as Narrative: Life through a Telescope

The above discussion is an attempt to show that the self is the genesis of the narrative, or that the event is implicit in its report. It is also an effort to separate the self from ethnicity, to demonstrate a way in which ethnicity is constructed. The narrative exists out of the self, and the report grows from the event; and although for many the production may not be obviously the fruit of its evolution, this is in fact what it is. The stories of the Inuit tribes of North America do not relate immediately to historic events, but they are a history related through the genre of the personified. Our feelings, narratives, and stories about our or others' ethnicity are similar to this. Each narrative has its history. The teller will relate it from his or her mind via memory, it will be distorted into a verbalization, and it might again be twisted to fit the symbolic confines of the written word. The person or audience to whom the narrative is offered will translate this product, and the original author will hand it over regarding his or her perception of the audience. At the same time, the narrative will have to be seen to be in the context of situational factors and will be created in a given social, economic, and cultural environment. It may be relayed into a similar environment or into an environment that has few if any of the same constituents of the environment of origin. Thus, the organization and interpretation of the narrative leave the original event behind. In the study of Gypsies, both academic and popularist, folk believe what they want to believe—see much of what they want to see.

Nietzsche (see Magee 1987, 234–37) suggests that we create values according to our needs, that different moralities are valid to different roles. It is possible that narratives of certain types (ethnicities) conveyed to a given community of interest will be interpreted according to the makeup of that community. For example, narratives of life in a women's prison given by the inmates will have similarities; if these are translated by feminists committed to prison reform, shared interpretations will be made. Likewise, if these narratives are picked up by supporters of the existing prison system, the shared interpretations would again exist, but would probably be of a different order, although even these disparate groups would share some conclusions. Nietzsche also thought that different civilizations have different knowledge. Indeed, it must be so that texts written two thousand years ago will be interpreted not according to the tenets of that age in which they were written. They will certainly be read in many different ways, each way giving a different interpretation. Hence, records concerning Gypsies written in the sixteenth century will not necessarily relate directly to our present understandings of those placed in this category today. However, some of these interpretations might be the same; some things may even have a similar meaning for all who interpret them at any given time. It is also true that each interpretation could add to what we call our understanding, even though each new perspective takes us further away from the actual event or the original meaning of the event. The literature relating to Gypsies can be criticized for not looking at the larger perspective; it expects, by looking at the Gypsy and his or her immediate situation, to understand the place of him or her in the universe throughout time. Those who live a Gypsy lifestyle may be passionate about the situation of Gypsies, but are they seeing the situation of Gypsies, or is what they are experiencing something more immediate than this? According to Hall, the analysis is not as clear as surface impressions formed in a particular social and historical moment might lead the observer to believe:

> *Identity is not as transparent or unproblematic as we think. Perhaps instead of thinking of identity as an already accomplished fact, which the new cultural practices then represent, we should think, instead, of identity as a "production," which is never complete, always in process, and always constituted within, not outside, representation.* (Hall 1990, 222)

We Are Narrative, We Are Selves

I want to conclude this section by arguing that just as we see the star through the telescope in the context of all the heavens—but cannot experience this world at first hand—so the narrative bequeaths to us the life.

The interactions of humanity can be seen as constantly creating novel perspectives on given Gypsy lives or events. Each new perspective shows us more of the object that is the life or the event, not as it was but as it is. Nietzsche might well have been hinting at this in his hope that the unrepressed person would be able to reevaluate his or her values. The metaphor (used by Nietzsche; see Magee 1987) of each event being lived again and again seems to be saying that the process of change through reflection is always necessary if we are to progress. The narrative transformed from the event, being the precursor to other events, is perhaps this active reflection and process of refining our actions that provides us with the opportunity for understanding of self-identity and ethnicity.

It would seem that we are things of narrative, made up of constant reevaluations, referring to narratives and having our own narratives analyzed by others. However, that which we call the self is not a narrative, but narratives of it are our means of accessing it, our pathway to understanding and developing it. Does this mean that self is narrative, in that the only material object we have is the narrative? Schopenhauer (1818; see Flew 2002) supplies one answer in presenting the person as a whole entity that can be seen from and through different perspectives of body or will. The will distorts the self of the phenomenal world (Freud was to be influenced by this view), art being the only escape from the rule of the will. We can use this theory by portraying a person as the creation of a self-narrative, which is the product of a complementary dialogue, wherein the self generates narrative and narrative elaborates the self. For Gypsies, the constant reinterpretation creates a picture that includes the world in which the total message is received and transmitted. Like the construct of the interactionists' self, there is a nondualistic fusion of two elements. Also similar to the interactionists' model, elements interact, but unlike the interactionist construct, within this device one element is essentially passive while the other is active.

This situates the self in relation to the narrative. We have lost the pure self, but we have something that may be more than this. Although this conscious loss of the bonafide self may lead us to reconstruct every notion we have regarding interviews, accuracy, and truth, and we may have to abandon the hope that we can ever clean up self-reports to the extent that we have a thoroughly hygienic social science, this may be our only conclusion. The aim has been to prevent narrative from being too dominant in a collective form that could overdetermine individual responses. In the last analysis, there is a fundamental problem:

> *The Jew is one whom other men consider a Jew: that is the simple truth from which we must start. . . . It is the anti-Semite who makes the Jew.* (Sartre in Fanon 1952, 92–93)

Conclusion

Narrative is a truth, not *the* truth. The nature of narrative is that it tells us something about the character of lives lived and how they are shaped in society and not how society is or lives actually are. This has been illustrated in a very concrete way by the product of the writing and research focusing on Gypsies. Okely points out that responses made by Gypsies are not always reliable:

> *I suggest that Travelers or Gypsies respond to the perceived preferences and values of gorgios . . . when it comes to elaborating their historical origins. There is a neat overlap between the claims of many non-Travelers and Travelers on this question. Malinowski (1931), the anthropologist, long ago suggested that peoples may recount and elaborate on myths of origin in order to validate their current status. The peoples he studied used origin myths to confirm hierarchy or difference.* (1994, 12)

As such, the power and ubiquitous nature of the ethnic narrative cannot be underestimated:

> *Travelers respond to the mythical origin which most suits non-Travelers.* (16)

The response Gypsies make to those intervening or interfering in their lives may not only be tainted by what they see as the wants and needs of the researcher. Feelings about their own position might not facilitate a clear reflection of their situation:

> *Gypsies who presented themselves as victims of members of their own nation or as drop-outs from the dominant "superior race" would appear to question the values of those in power and those with whom they had a supposed "natural" affinity. Much better if . . . Gypsies could be said to be descendents of exotic outsiders who had migrated.* (15)

The response given by Gypsies is also as fragile as the reaction of any respondent to the gaze of research:

> *The way Travelers choose to describe themselves to outsiders depends on who is asking the questions, what the context is, and what the Travelers stand to gain or lose by the labels.* (11)

As such, narratives—the stories of how people's lives are—are products of social interaction, a transmitter in relationship to a receiver. What we end up seeing is imbued by that relationship, so we see more than a set of neutral facts or an objective analysis of lives lived. What the narrative gives us is something deeply subjective and very much a product of the nature of society and the interactions that take place within the social milieu. The strength of the research presented in this book is that its narrative content is the product of curiosity, albeit of a rather structured kind. The perspectives collected between these covers were gathered not by a researcher from respondents; they are the products of real relationships and actual conversations, real and vibrant interactions of social equals.

In this chapter, I have complemented the essentially structuralist analysis of inclusion and exclusion of the previous chapter with the psychosocial perspective offered by the symbolic interactionist standpoint (Mead 1934a) in order to demonstrate the role of the self and other selves in the production of ethnic categories. This has been carried out to further demonstrate that ethnicity in general and Gypsy identity in particular is not a biological or racial phenomenon, but rather a product of social and human interaction. I have suggested that there exists an ethnic narrative relating to Gypsies and that this has been and is an influential force in terms of the general understanding of the Gypsy population.

7

Colonialism and the Gypsies

In this chapter, I will argue that the colonial narrative is effectively applied to the narrative of Gypsy ethnicity and that this collision of narratives gives rise to the social phenomenon that society recognizes as the Gypsy population. This group can then be treated and recognized according to its narration, which is confirmed and strengthened (as a truth) in the process.

Narrative is not just a positive or even neutral story. The narrative of the colonial situation, for example, places one group in the role of the oppressed and another group in a dominating position. This colonial narrative is deeply influential in the lives of those bound to it. The narrative of Gypsy ethnicity might be understood to exist within a broader colonial narrative of this type. Franz Fanon argues that the colonized are defined by and dependent on the definition of the colonizer. He discusses the way in which a group of people become defined by another (an outsider group) to the extent that their whole self and understanding of their humanity is dependent on that definition. Fanon points out that once people become dependent on this definition from another—from the outsider—they begin to live in order to fulfill that definition; they become as the oppressor would have them become:

> *Man is only human to the extent to which he tries to impose his existence on another man in order to be recognised by him. As long as*

> *he has not been effectively recognised by the other, that other will remain the theme of his actions. It is on that other being, on recognition by that other being, that his own human worth and reality depend. It is that other being in whom the meaning of his life is condensed.* (1965, 217)

Collaborative Categorization

This interaction creates all sorts of complex interactions. As a child, I recall being known by my family name: "He's a Belton." It meant several things. But most of all it meant I was only like a certain group of other people. I was not me; I was of them. The label applied to different things at different times, but in the main it implied that I was a member of a kind of pirate caste to be feared, distrusted, avoided, befriended, admired, respected, despised, or targeted, among other things. By the time I was twelve or thirteen, I had adopted this confused and contradictory persona. To an extent I had been made, and the response to me was, in the main, objectified. I was a Gypsy, a gangster, a yob, a hooligan, a troublemaker, a clown. But it was also known that I was intelligent, clever, and talented. Schoolwork was a breeze; I was always at the top of my class, all the time taking the piss out of the system and my teachers, who tried every way, from pleading to beating, to bridle my ability and focus on something, anything. It didn't work. I had been placed in Burke Secondary Modern School, the educational dumping ground of the London Borough of Newham, at a time when that local authority vied with Barking for the lowest secondary educational attainment in Britain, during a period when the United Kingdom was the lowest-achieving nation in Western Europe when it came to that particular educational sector (I went to the worst school in Western Europe!). Yet the good teachers who every day fought stoically against the odds in Burke (and they were good, coming from every corner of the planet to test their mettle against the challenge of east London) were exasperated. In my final year at school, with ease I topped the academic tree of Burke. I was invited back a year later to receive my prize for being one of the best scholars that battling institution had produced. My headmaster, Mr. Nobby Clarke, in front of the gathered parents and pupils, none of whom had done as well as "Bad Boy Belton," expectantly asked me what I was doing for a living. He really wanted to see me be the one to break the mold. This man, against the advice of all his colleagues, had seen to it that I was allowed to stay in education until I was sixteen (a decision that both mystified and met with the disapproval of my family), because he had taught my father during the years of World War II. With the brutal pleasure of the self-destructive, I announced that I was laboring in a sheet metal warehouse. Mr. Clarke hung his head and mumbled, "I see."

My adolescence was made up of violence, earning money to spend on clothes, jewelry, reggae, and following the West Ham United football team to every washed-out and rail-end town on the sodden map of what seemed to be a perpetually wintered Britain. I spent my time, in one way or another, telling the world to fuck off and that I didn't give a shit. I marked myself as irremediable and irreconcilable, living by the words of Pete Townsend, "I hope I die before I get old," and envied the Millwall (West Ham's East End rivals) dictum, "Nobody likes us, and we don't care." My Gypsyness fit in nicely with this. You, the gorgios, had it in for me; your nameless persecution of me was one of many excuses for me to shaft you and what belonged to you. You owed me, which meant that I agreed that you actually had everything. All that belonged to me were my Dr. Martens boots, my braces (suspenders), my stay-press trousers, my Ben Sherman, my music, the money in my pocket, and being West Ham. Most of that could not be taken away on any more than a temporary basis; for instance, when they arrested someone, the police would confiscate the laces from one's boots and confiscate those flimsy red, blue, or black braces; that attempt to undermine my identity always pleased and amused me. It was the best "old Bill" could do. However, these actions exemplified that I, to the world, was an object before I was a person. And by my actions I agreed with this; I played the role I was given, a willing collaborator within the process of my own dehumanization. I insisted I was different; I protested it, and I made the accusation that I was shit a reality. Just as those who promote the notion of race, even though they might be demanding racial equality, acquiesce with the eugenicists, those who invented race as a justification of slavery, I followed the path laid down for me by those who had shown nothing but contempt for my humanity, those who had labeled and categorized me. To that extent, I was colonized.

Fanon and Colonization

Franz Fanon (1965, 1967) addresses the issue of colonialism. Fanon provides a detailed scientific and theoretical account of the process of colonialism on the colonized. He outlines what might be thought of as the colonial mentality, through an analysis of the colonial neurosis (1965, 83–108). For Fanon,

> *The central idea is that the confrontation of "civilized" and "primitive" men creates a special situation—the colonial situation—and brings about the emergence of a mass of illusions and misunderstandings that only a psychological analysis can place and define.* (1965, 65)

According to Fanon, colonialism establishes a relationship between the oppressor and the oppressed that is founded on an assumption of the inferiority of the oppressed group and superiority of those who make up the oppressing elite (Jinadu 1986, 28–30). He argues that this relationship becomes part of the mentality of the oppressed to the extent that they are only able to perceive themselves as they are portrayed or understood to be by the oppressing group. It can be seen to be the case that this analysis is applicable to Gypsies who define themselves according to official, academic, or popular romantic stereotypes. According to Fanon, the oppressed become trapped in this definition of their selves. Fanon argues that this is a dehumanizing process; the oppressed are not regarded as fully human, by themselves or the oppressor; they define themselves and are defined as "the other." Only the oppressor is wholly human. This was the experience I lived. While writing this book I was shown a promotion for a talk being given by Ian Hancock, the Gypsy theorist. It claimed that he was going to talk about something like the unique experience of being a Gypsy. However, I doubt if Fanon was mentioned, let alone how definers like Hancock are, albeit unwittingly, part of the endemic spread of the colonial mentality.

The fundamental problem with calling someone (or oneself) a Gypsy is that human identity takes on a secondary status; one is first a Gypsy, a type with traits that differentiate and alienate the individual from the whole. The only way out of this situation is to move back into the mainstream through forms of social compliance and conformity to particular norms. Fanon argues that the mechanisms of adaptation and imitation within the colonial relationship are often very subtle. Certain norms are established and imposed to which the oppressed group is then required to conform to by law. Assimilation is an example of this kind of imitation imposed by the colonial elite (maybe through leadership or activity connected to Gypsy issues—which, by their very existence, will confirm the identity). For Fanon, these mechanisms can also be overt and deliberately instituted, with sanctions stipulated by the oppressing group.

While the first example of imitation (subtle) seems spontaneous, the second (overt) is induced. For Fanon,

> The arrival of the white man in Madagascar shattered not only its horizons but its psychological mechanisms. . . . An island like Madagascar invaded overnight by "pioneers of civilization," even if those pioneers conducted themselves as well as they knew how, suffered the loss of its basic structure. . . . The landing of the white man on Madagascar inflicted injury without measure. The consequences of the interruption of Europeans onto Madagascar were not psychological alone, since, every authority has observed, there are inner relationships between consciousness and the social context. (1965, 97)

This process is not too far from that experience within the relationship between Gypsies and the state. The invasion of Gypsy lifestyle, by the means of social pressure and force of law (see Hancock 1987), is undertaken in order to oblige Gypsies to comply with social norms. The less the Gypsy conforms, the more he or she will remain confined within the characterization of the Gypsy and suffer the consequences. Fanon states:

> *I begin to suffer from not being a white man to the degree that the white man imposes discrimination on me, makes me a colonized native, robs me of all worth, all individuality, tells me that I am a parasite on the world, and that I must bring myself as quickly as possible into step with the white world.* (1965, 98)

According to Fanon, the urge to become like the oppressor (white) and cultured leads the acculturated colonial subject to despise those less fortunate in his society. This might be understood in the Gypsy context as being similar to the negative feelings so-called pure Gypsies (true Romanies) have toward other traveling groups, in particular New Age Travelers (see Hetherington 2000, 132). Thus, Gypsies can be understood to be bound up in a colonial narrative that can only be compounded by the notion of Gypsy ethnicity. The means to address this situation seems to lie in the development of a more accurate, rational understanding of the nature of the Gypsy population not based on traditional romanticism or contemporary notions of ethnicity. The Gypsy persona as the other needs to be challenged by an analysis that can accommodate the means by which the Gypsy population arises out of the social and economic fabric of the state. As far as Gypsies are concerned this amounts to a discourse of deconstruction. However, for the moment I will look further at the similarity between the position of Gypsies in contemporary society and those oppressed under a colonial regime.

The African Simile

Kuper and Smith's analysis of pluralism in Africa (1971) provokes comparison with the position of Gypsies in contemporary Western society. Kuper and Smith look at the experience of colonization, particularly in respect to the postcolonial situation in

Africa, and seek to demonstrate how economic relations can play a critical role in creating notions of difference, a role that can be understood to preempt race, culture, or ethnicity. This illustrates a theoretical precedent for the analysis presented in this book.

Many of the cultural expressions used by Gypsies in modern Western society can be seen to have historical precedent within the African colonial and postcolonial situation. For example, the use of music, dance, and protest in the so-called New Age groups (Earle et al. 1994; McKay 1996, 7, 127–58) and the emergence of a pidgin language (McKay 1996, 138, 331–32, 310; Okely 1983, 6–13) in more traditional populations have correspondences in the African context (M. Smith 1971b, 153–65). The colonial expression of these areas grew out of the gaps that were left between the planks of colonial power in Africa and in many cases took on the energy out of which liberation from oppression eventually took (and takes) place.

As such, a conceptual relationship can be developed between the colonial experience and the modern incarnation of Gypsy culture. This arises out of similar social interactions that echo the inequality of the pre- and postcolonial situation. Gypsy cultural affinities, practices, and mythologies, which result out of certain social and psychological conditions, resemble those erupting out of the experience of colonization so closely that one is obliged to consider the notion of the Gypsy as being a direct product of a colonized population. As part of this analysis, which provides further explanation of the nature and source of Gypsy identity, connection by way of a genetic or biological typology is questioned, as are ethnic or racial linkages derived from ideas about language, customs, and rites.

Kuper and Smith write about plural societies. These societies, although brought together in a single political unit, are characterized by sharp cleavages that exist between different sections of the population. In such a context pluralism results in dissention between groups based on racial, tribal, regional, or religions differences. Under these circumstances, regulation and force maintain the system (1971, 3–5). A tradition that is antithetical to this situation is the society wherein there is a dispersion of power between groups that, through overlapping loyalties, common values, or a competitive balance of power, bind the society together.

For Kuper and Smith, the colonial society might be understood as a plural society. Such an environment can be seen to have emerged in a wide range of locations around the world after the enforced adoption of the European market system through the imposition of colonization (Kuper 1971, 11, 14; M. Smith 1971a, 36; van den Berghe 1971, 73). In such situations people of different ethnic origin only met in the context of the market. Out of this contorted social climate a new type of society arose, alongside the expansion of trade that generated a unique market situation. In this new market, the participants had no common values, customs, or social institutions. Individuals were separated into discrete groups in all but economic activities. The resultant market society lacked the social protections of Western capitalist society. This lack of social constraints allowed a much more intensive pursuit of individual self-interest and a greater level of exploitation relative to the West. Those of different ethnic groups than the colonizing group were the focus of exploitation. This analysis shows a relationship between market systems, culture, and community and suggests that the separation of these, as much as the cleavages between ethnic groups, creates pluralness.

There exists within this model an attempt to understand racial divisions in the light of prevailing social conditions (those of colonial society). What is being said is that racial divisions are dependent on something other than purely racial differences for their creation and maintenance. The social position of Gypsies in contemporary society can be seen to have a striking resemblance to that of the colonized people. Gypsies, as a group, are portrayed as having a range of distinct values, the makeup and order of which differs from those of non-Gypsies (see, for example, Fraser 1992; Okely 1983). Generally speaking, Gypsies are seen as not sharing in the institutional framework of non-Gypsies and are thought to have established customs that are unique to a Gypsy culture. They are categorized as being different from non-Gypsies, yet both Gypsies and non-Gypsies are considered to be a single political unit.

Conflict and dissension exists both among people with a background premised on iterant ways of life—New Age, Gypsies, Romanies, Tinkers, and so on (see Okely in Rehfisch and Rehfisch 1975, 59–63; Hawes and Perez 1995, 6)—and between Gypsies and non-Gypsies. Interactions between these groups, from differing affinities are, in the main, restricted to market relations (for example, see Southwark Traveller Women's Group 1992, 52). Far and away the market is the most common venue for interaction between Gypsies and non-Gypsies (work, selling, access to welfare: see Okely 1983, 49–50). Like colonized people, Gypsies enter the market without the protections afforded non-Gypsies (often working in the alternative economy in casual employment; see Okely 1983, 126–27, 140, 145, 181). Relative to the colonial situation, Gypsies suffer similar forms of exploitation in terms of conditions, pay, and restrictions imposed on where and when they are allowed to take part in the process of exchange.

Looked at in this way, it can be understood that a Gypsy way of life, like race in the colonial situation, is but a mark of exploitation. What maintains the divisions that exist between Gypsies and non-Gypsies, what in a sense gives rise to the distinct cultural expressions of Gypsies, is a particular position in the market situation. This perspective seems to confirm a Marxist analysis that ethnic divisions are epiphenomena of the economic makeup of society. For Marx, the human essence is a social, historical construction, being the product of a collection of social relations (Malik 1996, 237). This has certainly been confirmed by my own Gypsy life. I have moved from the position of being, by definition, a different type of human being to being a human who sees things differently, not because of what I am, but who I am, not only defined by where I come from but also by where I have been and might go. This is what it means to be acknowledged as a whole person, something more than a person who is more or less judged (by themselves and others) as being preeminently a Gypsy.

For Marxist thought, social class exists when individuals who perform like functions in the production process become aware of their common interests and unify in the promotion of these interests against the opposing class (see Miles 1989, 110). This solidarity among workers is undermined when workers from a dominant section perform a different function in the production process; that is, they make up an aristocracy of labor. To an extent this is the situation in plural societies and the basis of the division that exists between Gypsies and non-Gypsies in contemporary Western society. The aristocracy of labor in Western society is dominated by non-Gypsies (see, for example, Okely 1994, 4, 12; O'Connell 1994, 117; McCarthy 1994, 123). Their privileged position is derived from their relative political power, even in situations where Gypsies and non-Gypsies perform similar functions in the process of production (Okely 1994, 5; McLoughlin 1994, 81–82). For instance, a mechanic who is a Gypsy is likely to be operating in the alternative economy, in casual employment. As such, he or she is unprotected by, for example, employment or health and safety legislation. However, a mechanic from a non-Gypsy background is more likely to be found in legitimate employment with all the incumbent rights that accompany the same.

In plural societies, race can become a social category and race relations become hierarchical via the elaboration of racial differences as a principle of organization and association in political and other institutions. In terms of Western society, Gypsies have become a social category, and relations have become hierarchical through the defining of lifestyle differences as a principle of organization and association in all institutions.

In the colonized society, these functions bestow an independent significance on race. Economic position is merely one of the associated factors. Racial domination provides the cement for interclass solidarity inside the dominant section. Even if some measure of solidarity exists across racial divisions, this is suffocated by the overarching racial solidarity. For the subordinate section, the common oppression by the dominant group is experienced as a totality and creates a racial response that overrides class divisions. This mechanism fits the contemporary academic view of Gypsy politics. Non-Gypsies are depicted as a homogenous group (regardless of class position) that oppresses Gypsies. This oppression is the binding that holds the category of Gypsy (regardless of class position) together (see Weber 1922).

As such, ethnic and cultural diversity and an unequal distribution of political power, coupled with the discriminatory effects on the subordinate group, including the effects of legislation, succeed in masking the common class interests. This being the case, racism or cultural categorization (division) continues. Thus, while Western society continues to follow the sociocultural explanations in seeking to address issues affecting Gypsies and perhaps any other ethnic group, it will continue to be bound into a kind of discriminatory loop, whose effect is to divert attention away from the underlying contradictions and exploitation indicative of a capitalist market economy. This book is a plea to consider a broader explanatory plan, taking in, particularly, the effects of the sociopolitical character of society, the context within which Gypsies and non-Gypsies exist. It is certain that legislation affecting Gypsies emanates from the same. As such, any explanation that fails to analyze the political relationship that Gypsies have to the rest of society and their purpose within this is at best partial, merely adding to the confusion and mystification surrounding Gypsies. At worst, in an insistence on restricted racial or ethnic focus, it is a species of racism.

Conclusion

In this chapter, I have followed the examination of the role of narrative (Scheibe 1986) from the last chapter, using a Fanonian (Fanon 1952, 1961) analysis to construct a theory of a colonial narrative of Gypsy ethnicity. I have pointed out the similarity between the social positions of Gypsies and the colonized groups in the African pluralist societies. This again demonstrates how the ethnicity-generating forces arise out of social and economic relations.

The combined analysis of this and previous chapters provides an alternative view, relative to the fundamentally racial model found in the literature, of how Gypsy ethnicity might be developed and maintained. I have argued that ethnicity is a notion rather than an indisputable, concrete phenomenon. I have suggested that, at least in part, Gypsy identity has arisen and develops out of social action, interaction, and the general socioeconomic environment. Ethnicity then can be understood as being defined by the self in cooperation and in conjunction with other selves, importantly within historically and socially specific terms of reference.

Following this chapter, ethnicity can now be recognized as an ethnic narrative. This can be used to analyze the meaning of ethnicity: why and how the notion of ethnicity is deployed and maintained within general social discourse to preserve an ethnic and cultural roots version of Gypsy identity. This book is a critique of this moribund position, providing a broader view of the nature and generation of Gypsy identity, that gives much more consideration to the social imperatives affecting those labeled as Gypsy. It has shown how social interaction and conditions might contribute to the development and expansion of the Gypsy population. This has been undertaken in order to offer an alternative or supplementary explanation to that provided in the general body of literature relating to Gypsies.

8

Defining Legislation

In this chapter, I will illustrate how legislative activity can be understood to motivate the formation of a Gypsy ethnicity through the identification and isolation of a marginalized group. This gives rise to the adoption of defense strategies by this population in the face of oppressive legislation. This demonstrates a dual process of ethnicity building that is generated by means of legislative conferment and defensive adoption.

I will suggest that the character of the legislation demonstrates the operation of Foucault's notion of the carceral (1977, 293–308). I will argue that ethnicity, along with its narrative and sentimental attachments, is used as a means of social control and regulation of Gypsies.

Hancock (1987) has shown at some length how the force of law has been a consistent facet of Gypsy experience in the United States. Other writers have also highlighted the persistent and concentrated effect of legislation on Gypsies (see, for example, Okely 1975; 1983, 20–21; Acton 1974; Adams et al. 1974; Hawes and Perez 1995; Fraser 1992, 2–3) that effectively acts as a deterrent to an existence based on traveling and temporary work, lifestyles that depart from social and market norms.

Although harassment has been a feature of the response to Gypsies, it would be too simplistic to argue that this has taken place as an end in itself, as has been claimed in the literature.

However, I have shown that this group is likely to include many who come from non-Gypsy backgrounds, and as such it is the essential element of control that is fundamental to understanding the nature of the legislation affecting Gypsies.

In the literature referring to Gypsies, human agency is described in terms of the psychology of discrimination and prejudice. These phenomena are seen as key factors in the framing of legislation. For example:

> *We set modern responses against an historic backdrop, in the hope of illustrating somewhat deeper arguments about the process by which prejudice, fear, and antagonism to minority peoples becomes fixed in the formal structures of society.* (Hawes and Perez 1995, 9)

This exemplifies the neglect of a broad sociological perspective in the literature. In this chapter, I want to address this by providing an analysis of social mechanisms that drive the social responses framed in legislation that have an impact on Gypsies. The following will suggest that the social formation will move to eliminate structures outside of its logic, the logic of the current social formation being that of capitalism. It will control, via law that is framed in the interests of capital, structures or movements that contravene market norms. Gypsies are thus the focus of legislation and harassment because they reject a range of market norms—for example, employment and housing. It is not psychological dispositions that give rise to social responses to Gypsies; legislation is not just a matter of will or a general attitude. Marx's analysis suggests,

> *In the social production of their life, men enter into definite relations that are indispensable and independent of their will, relations of production which correspond to a definite stage of development of their material productive forces. The sum total of these relations of production constitutes the economic structure of society, the real foundation, on which rises a legal and political superstructure and to which correspond definite forms of social consciousness. The mode of production of material life conditions the social, political, and intellectual life process in general. It is not the consciousness of men that determines their being, but, on the contrary, their social*

being that determines their consciousness. (Marx, K., quoted in Carver 1982, 22)

For Marx, social being determines consciousness. Marx was drawing on the Hegelian dialectic, an important factor in shaping thinking about the modern notion of the individual. The notion is that as soon as one begins to define oneself as an individual, isolated and separate, one needs to exclude something else (see Marcuse 1968, 389–98; Carver 1982, 45–48; Brewer 1984, 2, 185). In the end, this process of exclusion becomes so crucial—because identity is dependent on it—the individual (as has been demonstrated in previous chapters of this book) becomes understood as the product of the other.

We are moved as a society and as individuals by great social events, wars, revolutions, and social conditions that affect masses of people in profound and lasting ways; these have an impact on housing, employment, and economic institutions. The extent of this is well elaborated by Bertolt Brecht's Mother Courage, the seminal figure in his play *Mother Courage and Her Children* (1983). She thinks she is choosing; she thinks she is making her life; but in fact she is being absolutely destroyed and pulled apart by great historical contradictions. Maybe this is the human consequence of Marx's insight. The narratives I have cited in other chapters demonstrate that this is partly understood by people, at an instinctive level. Expressions like "I am what I am" are premised or followed by statements about being something of a cork on a social sea.

> *I am a Gypsy. I was born a Gypsy. I decide where I want to go and what I want to do. I'm proud of that. You got to be how you are. People know what you are. You might pretend to be something else, but they recognize you: and you are as the world sees you. Let's face it: what we are is how others see us. I don't care what other people think, but even if I did it wouldn't matter. I know an Indian guy, says he's Italian. But he can say that as much as he wants, he's still an Indian. That's what people say he is. Maybe he's an Italian Indian.* (Ralph, Nashville)

According to Marx, it is the "economic structure of society" that is "the real foundation on which rises the legal and political superstructure." However, the idea that the character of society is fundamental to what happens in society is of course not just a Marxist concept; indeed, it is a basic tenet of most sociology, be it Marxist, Weberian, or Durkheimian. The notion that society and its legal and political superstructure are built by or on psychological, attitudinal forces of individuals has a conservative, right-wing ancestry:

> *The State as conceived and realized by fascism is a spiritual and ethical entity for securing the political, juridical, and economic organization of the nation, an organization which in its origin and growth is a manifestation of the Spirit. . . . Far from crushing the individual, the Fascist State multiplies his energies, just as in a regiment a soldier is not diminished but multiplied by the number of his fellow soldiers.* (Mussolini 1935, 27–29)

If one sees legislation affecting Gypsies as being possibly derived from the spiritual or ethical premises, as put forward by the likes of Hawes and Perez (1995), then this means seeing society ordered in much the same way as Mussolini describes. However, according to Marx society does not rest upon law, because

> *this is a juridical function. Just the reverse is the truth. Law rests on society; it must be the expression of the general interest that springs from the material production of a given society against the arbitrariness of any single individual.*
>
> *Here, the code of laws which I hold in my hands has not created modern civil society. It happened just the other way. The civil society . . . found its legal expression in the code. As soon as it ceases to correspond with the social conditions, the code will be as effete as waste paper.* (Marx 1849, in Meyer 1954, 8)

Taking this into consideration, it can be understood that legislation affecting Gypsies is the legal expression of society and corresponds to social conditions that are capitalist in character.

> *Men do not make their own history . . . not just as they please; they do not make it under circumstances chosen by themselves, but under circumstances directly found, given, and transmitted from the past.* (Marx 1935, 13)

Defining Legislation / 151

The next section will expand on this perspective via the thought of Michael Foucault. It will argue that the legislation affecting Gypsies, being essentially a part of the general social process of control and discipline, elaborates, exemplifies, complements, and confirms the nature of the social form in which it is wrought.

Foucault and Genealogy

The force of narrative is that it frees us from the confines of what I like to call ordinary history. Ordinary history ties us to the facts remarked on from geographical, psychic, emotional, or spiritual distance. According to McNay (1994, 88), Michel Foucault sees traditional historiography as representing the passage of time as a logical stream of causally linked events, each event having a discrete significance helping to form part of the greater pattern of meaning that is history. This is what Foucault describes as a "formless unity of a great becoming" (1972, 55). For Foucault, these events are slotted into an all-embracing explanation of things, producing an artificial unity. What could be called the conventional view of Gypsy history and the identity arising out of this might be understood to exemplify this process. According to Foucault, this teleological interpretation deprives events of their uniqueness and immediacy. For him,

> *The world we know is not this ultimately simple configuration where events are reduced to accentuate their essential traits, their final meaning, or their initial and final value. On the contrary, it is a profusion of entangled events.* (1986, 89)

So, for Foucault, Gypsy identity and history need to be understood as the product of a vast complexity of events, situations, and incidents and not the type of linear formation suggested by, for example, Fraser (1992). Foucault perceives history in its traditional translation as a lie, highlighting seminal moments and at the same time placing the self-reflexive subject in the middle of the flow of history. It is the human character that becomes central to the movement of history; it is this that is driven by the merged consciousness of humanity; history becomes an interpretation and playing out of human nature within the changing context of society. However, Gypsies settle, and the settled take up traveling; individuals exchange communities and cultures. This occurs as a result of the impact of economic or social considerations on individuals, families, or groups. It is the collective effect of this intermingling and interchange that for Foucault drives the historical process.

At any time or place, the particular circumstances give rise to the emergence of a Gypsy population. Thus, there would be, for Foucault, any number of Gypsy histories and identities. However, the recording of history is carried out in what McNay (1994, 89) calls "a logic of identity." For him,

History is read narcissistically to reconfirm one's present sense of identity, and any potentially disruptive awareness of alterity is suppressed. (McNay 1994; see also Foucault 1986, 84–85)

The analysis of the Gypsy population offered by much of the literature appertaining to Gypsies (for example, Hancock 1987) exemplifies the type of response that McNay (and Foucault) critique. It is what Foucault would see as traditional historiography. Human characteristics are placed at the center of historical processes. Psychological intention, discrimination, and sentiment are portrayed as the forces that define Gypsies, their activity, and what happens to them. It takes the situation of Gypsies at face value and builds an analysis on the basis of prescribed identities, Gypsy/non-Gypsy. Accusations by theorists that provoke resentment on the part of Gypsies and guilt in non-Gypsies and bind them together in a blinkered perspective that clinically isolates the Gypsy population as a discrete ethnicity or race. At the same time, this group is cut off from wider social issues, roots, interaction, and causation.

In an attempt to address this problem of cultural discrimination, I employ Foucault's use of the Nietzschian idea of effective history or genealogy linked to a notion of analysis of descent or emergence. Events emerge by chance within the process of history in a discontinuous and divergent manner. Genealogy, "the philosophy of the event" (McNay 1994, 89), is the analytical method that follows the disruptive and erratic dispersion of processes, which overlap and accrue, that give rise to the event. A genealogical analysis of the Gypsy population would understand this phenomenon as arising out of a complexity of social interactions and conditions, which themselves are subject to chaotic ebb and flow. This population would also need to be comprehended as a complicated mixture of groups, prone to change and flux, like everything else, in a constant state of emergence or becoming. Thus, we can never say definitively what the Gypsy population is or who they are. However, at any given time their presence has a meaning. This echoes the thoughts of Pico Della Mirandola (1463–94), who undertook the great oration *On the Dignity of Man* (1965), one of the seminal humanist texts of the Renaissance concept of humanity, which argues that God did not make human beings fixed, but fluid and changing. Conditions, events, and situations and our response to the same provoke and stimulate our propensity to adapt behaviorally, culturally, and socially. It is precisely because we are mobile that we move between identities; this is something that arises out of being human and has been shown in the narratives that I have presented in this book. Anything that impedes this development, that categorizes by force of law or even academic practice, for example, is inhumane.

This perspective is the antithesis of the contention that a secure connecting line of Gypsy identity or ethnicity exists and that this joins current Gypsies living in America to traveling groups emanating from Asia hundreds or even thousands of years ago.

The concepts of power and the body derive from the notion of genealogical analysis. Foucault utilizes Nietzsche's idea that force has primacy over meaning, seeing that history is a result of an ongoing battle between power interests that seek to dominate. For him,

> *Humanity does not gradually progress from combat to combat until it arrives at universal reciprocity, where the rule of law finally replaces warfare; humanity installs each of its violences in a system of*

rules and thus proceeds from domination to domination. (Foucault 1986, 85)

This being the case, history becomes the playing out of a sequence of violence. From this standpoint, the contemporary position of and perspective on Gypsies can be understood to emerge from a stream of legislation aimed at promoting market and social norms. The power interests that are expressed in this relationship seek to dominate through the establishment and enforcement of these norms.

Although Foucault sees the orthodox Marxist analysis of power relations—being set in the economy and class conflict—as a functionalist oversimplification (McNay 1994, 91), a slightly more complex application of the same enables the Gypsy population to be understood, at least in part, as a phenomenon arising out of a conflict or contradiction within capital. This contradiction gives rise to groups that are unable or unwilling to respond to the market; at the same time, it creates legitimate forms of violence (of which the state has a monopoly) with the purpose of bringing about conformity to the existing social and market (the two cannot be separated in a capitalist society) norms.

The Knife, the Carceral

The violent tool of history helps categorize and abstract the individual. The potential damage this does to an individual and those around him or her is exemplified in the experience of the self-colonized. The consequence of this violence emerges in the course of life (see chapter 7).

The ethos of control necessarily permeates to and from the smallest incidents and encounters; it has no beginning or end; it is ever present and everywhere. Law and legislation are its overall thematic, but it is deeply rooted in our personal and group confrontations with each other.

As a youth worker I have, for more than thirty years, been involved with Gypsies and have, I feel, experienced the reverberations of violent categorization of those thus labeled. I was, in the course of working with a site in North London, driving a group of young people to a theme park in Surrey. I knew the group pretty well and that they had no reference points relative to such an experience; none of them had ever visited what to them was something akin to "Disneyland; like what you see on the telly." As such, the excitement in the minibus was tangible as we approached the park from the M25, the main London orbital road. We were moving at around 60 mph, in the fast lane, when Roll, one of the young men sitting behind me (I was driving), drew a large flick-knife across my throat. I felt the sharp blade push against my windpipe.

At the time, I was an experienced worker and, surprisingly enough I suppose, this was not the first time this had happened to me. What was strange was that Roll was silent: no shouting, no explanation, no demands. I was not scared or particularly anxious, but I was surprised and, rather perversely in retrospect, intrigued. There were a number of reasons for my lack of definite fear. As a young man I had been exposed to enough violence to be acclimatized to knives (as much as one can be), but also no one in the bus reacted to what was happening, although it seemed clear that at least six people were aware of the situation. The entire event lasted no more than a few seconds, but I remember thinking about what I should or could do, even though my response felt almost instantaneous and intuitive. The last time the same thing had happened to me I had just ignored it, carrying on with conversation, whistling, and asking my assailant (Kenny) to "leave under the nose . . . I'm growing a mustache" as if he were a barber shaving me. That made the incident almost comic and that had discharged the situation. However on that occasion I knew Kenny to be a very disturbed young man, whose life had been webbed together in a mesh of violence. But what was happening between Roll and me was qualitatively different. I knew that he was not where Kenny had been psychologically.

I swerved across the three lanes of the M25 onto the hard shoulder and slammed the bus to a halt and said:

Get the fuck off me now! *What the fuck are you doing?*

This was not part of a panic or a yell. It was a definite, firm instruction. I studied Roll's face in the rearview mirror. He looked surprised but not shocked. He glanced, as if puzzled, into the mirror. Our eyes met for a second and then his gaze moved to the reflection of the knife that was still held tight to my throat. In an instant the weapon disappeared into his pocket. There was a brief silence while everyone in the bus stared at me. I then moved back into the stream of traffic and continued to our destination. The noise and excitement quickly returned to its previous level.

Thinking about this incident later, and up to now, the best part of fifteen years on, I believe my response was something from me, the categorized Gypsy, responding to him, the categorized Gypsy. His knife was drawn to exemplify a difference, and my rejoinder worked to deny that difference. At the moment that the force of ordinary history provoked a reaction, I refused an invitation to be different. My insistence on our sameness, our shared primal, basic humanity, voiced in short, sincere, and authentic narrative, dislocated the violence. Looking back, I still believe that a brand of middle-class, white, professional rationality, some attempt to talk Roll down or my previous strategy, to ignore this powerful and intense gesture, would firstly have, as an intellectual attack, humiliated him, and secondly would have confirmed his instinctive understanding of the situation:

1. I (the youth worker/the professional/the outsider) was in control because
   a) I was driving the bus (the youth worker/professional/outsider was in control)
   b) I was taking them somewhere (they were going with me).
2. I was the source of the excitement (influence/power), which was in fact a vicious ruse in the process of colonization (I know he wouldn't have used that word or concept, but he would probably recognize the incumbent and associated feelings).

We all had a good day. Roll and I parted good friends, the incident was never mentioned, and we saw one another again a few times after our day together at the theme park and remained on good terms. But I still carry some uncomfortable feelings about that dramatic encounter between Roll and myself. If my judgment about what motivated Roll's moment of seeming aggression is accurate, I believe that his actions were explicable, understandable, and basically righteous. The aim of the work with him and the others had been to informally educate the group; that's what youth workers are funded to do: it is a process of covert indoctrination to promote conformity to state aims (control) that are presented as social values—a recognizable strategy of colonization. I was an agent of this and used myself, the me of me, to disarm his understandable defensive reaction to such violence; I took away his defense. This demonstrates the density of the tangled web of colonization and categorization and the seeming omnipresence of violence inherent in the carceral society.

Power and the Gypsy

For Foucault, at the heart of this warfare between power formations lies the human body. The forces of history act through and on the body in a way that cannot be understood from what McNay calls "a totalizing historical perspective" (1994, 89), the type of focus adopted by many theorists interested in Gypsy affairs (for example, Fraser 1992; Acton 1974; Hancock 1987). The body, for Foucault, is the most revealing tableau in terms of the exercise of power—it illustrates the nature of disciplinary power. The body is molded and remolded by the power blocs that are involved in the constant conflict that constitutes history. Foucault states:

> *The body is the inscribed surface of events (traced by language and dissolved by ideas), the locus of a dissociated self (adopting the illustration of a substantial unity), and a volume in perpetual disintegration. Genealogy, as an analysis of descent, is thus situated within the articulation of the body and history. Its task is to expose a body totally imprinted by history and the process of history's destruction of the body.* (Foucault 1986, 83)

Here we see how power relations infuse every facet and level of social existence. The history of Gypsies presented in the literature is essentially teleological, tracing the origins of Gypsies along an ethnic, racial, or cultural path. What this book has tried to present is a more genealogical analysis, seeing the Gypsy population as a product of definite power relations that operate on a defined body (labeled Gypsy). The reader has been asked to consider the Gypsy as a body imprinted by history. In the process of history, the human body of the Gypsy has been destroyed, leaving nothing but the Gypsy. Thus, the power that isolates and oppresses the Gypsy derives from that label placed on the body. This person can be treated like this because he or she is a Gypsy. This application of power on the body is used by Gypsiologists (as exemplified by Hancock 1987). Such an analysis cannot regard legislation as the result of diverse and divergent events emerging out of the continuous struggle between various power blocs. Unlike Foucault, the literature concerning itself with Gypsies consistently suggests that power is exercised with intentionality, as a negative force of oppression, which is the property of an elite. Foucault, on the other hand, does not see power necessarily being applied from above, in Hawes and Perez's (1995) terms, by the State. According to Foucault, one needs to be involved with an "ascending analysis of power from below" (quoted in Gordon 1980, 102).

This being the case, laws affecting Gypsies can be understood as exemplifying the ongoing struggle of power within the social realm. Such legislation is partly energized by the accepted notion of the Gypsy, as applied to individual bodies. While the legislation has no necessary consistency, it does chart a line of interest or power obliging conformity to conventional market forms, consistent with the logic of capital.

Power, Knowledge, Truth, and the Prison

Foucault's (1977) ideas on the nature of the prison can be used to explore how the site or encampment, the archetypal residence of the Gypsy, can be understood as a form of discipline on the body of the Gypsy. The site (as referred to here) is not the place where the romantic nomad Gypsy lays camp. The site is the place where Gypsies are seen to belong. Throughout the

Western world, Gypsies are increasingly placed on fixed, permanent sites, stocked with immovable caravans, often patrolled by wardens, and set in the most undesirable of areas. They are, as such, the very antithesis to any idea of itinerancy (see Hyman 1989 and Belton 2005, for example). For all this, most of the literature appertaining to Gypsies promotes the idea that this is the ethnic locale of this group, and pressure for the right for Gypsy sites.

The Gypsy site can also be understood as a psychological location: a psychic disposition that looks like where Gypsies should be, but is actually a pastiche of a romantic ideal arising out of and related to an ethnic narrative. As fast as the site physically grows, it might be said that there is a complementary development in the mental site as Gypsy identity becomes established as an ethnic type.

Foucault (1977) argues that the prison is the most overt testimony of the disciplinary society. For him, the development of modern society has produced a situation wherein each individual has been objectified from this point and subjected to the manipulation of forces driven by a power-knowledge dynamic. The individual or group objectified as Gypsy emerges from this dynamic and thereafter is open to manipulation appropriate to this label.

For Foucault, there is no historical moment at which the prison erupts into existence. The prison, as we recognize it, is at once generated by and is instrumental in the creation and sustaining of contemporary society. Given the nature of society, the prison is a necessary and complementary artifact. We cannot escape from the prison; it at once accompanies and is of the prevailing social form. As we stare into the big-house, as we analyze what it means to be put away, according to Foucault, we translate the society we live in; we uncover its evolution and make manifest its inner rationale. The Gypsy site, which is a product of social forces, is another manifestation of this inner rationale.

This model is founded on a conception that knowledge is formed within a power system. Knowledge has to be accrued, communicated, and ordered. These mediating factors are invested with the prevailing dominant forms of power that in turn affect and create knowledge. As such, the person interpreted as a Gypsy has, in the process, been exposed to forms of power that infect the final object presented (the Gypsy). At the same time, any power is reliant on knowledge. What can be said about Gypsies is reliant on the knowledge of this category. Knowledge is a constituent factor of power, as applied in our society. Power is power because it applies knowledge in a characteristic manner to sustain the power structures. Sets of knowledge have to be gained, applied, and retained in order to deploy power. So, Gypsies are presented in the way that they are in order to complement existing formations of power. This relationship of power-knowledge forms the basic building blocks of the institutions that make up and dictate the character of modern society. What we call the Gypsy is the product of knowledge; they live in this or that way, they do A and not B. The category thus established is treated within the existing power system (which is a disciplinary system). The product of this is the site.

According to Foucault, an economy of truth dictates the nature of a society. This is arrived at via power-knowledge, that is, according to how knowledge of certain types is extracted, presented, and distributed, how an order is established between them, and how they operate socially. Truth is knowledge laundered by the prevailing articles of power: power saturated knowledge. This is the root of the fundamental flaw in much of the literature pertaining to Gypsies. It starts out as taking the Gypsy as a fact, an ethnic given. This, however, is knowledge mediated by existing power interests. At the same time, this truth produces forms of power. For example, Hawes and Perez (1995) confirm the fact of Gypsiness and the requirement of sites (as the site is taken to be the natural place for Gypsies). Any given form of power gives rise to a nexus of truth that is necessary and adequate to it, the truth as framed, for instance by Hawes and Perez (1995), while certain articulations of truth produce forms of power that are requisite to them; the way Gypsies are treated. This is Foucault's economy of power, a self-reinforcing mechanism that exists to perpetuate itself, a corollary to the mechanistic metaphor of capitalism. Thus, the analyst of power must refer to the knowledge(s) that are embedded in the mechanisms of power, while understanding that any knowledge is formed via these mechanisms. As such, in a system that promotes conventional forms of housing as the norm (housing that feeds or is set within the capitalist nexus), forms of housing that undermine this system cannot be sustained or tolerated. A certain species of truth is needed to accommodate this: for example, Gypsies naturally require sites; sites are linked to the ethnic and cultural drives of Gypsies; they need and want them.

For Foucault, the prison produces and applies knowledge and in turn implicates it to generate power. The prison is a power station, fueled by a hot core of knowledge. The human sciences emerge from the disciplinary social institutions (of which the prison is one) as the apex of the techniques of power therein employed. Foucault (1977) deploys a description of the generation of the prison as a power mechanism. A product of this was the criminal, the individual, isolated and so able to be observed, described on the basis of this observation and defined in terms of like individuals, the criminal population (knowledge). The criminal is thus understood according to a particular power context. This understanding will complement the power formation that created it. The criminal is thus a product of knowledge imbued with power. The Gypsy can be understood to be generated in a similar manner through the site. So the existence of the Gypsy produces sites, and sites confirm the existence of Gypsies.

Foucault portrays the prison in a whole landscape of power-knowledge. The site can be understood as part of this. The rationale of this panorama is to take the individual identified as deviant or abnormal through "coercion by means of observation" (Foucault 1977, 170–71) and, in the case of Gypsies, assign them to the site—via categorization. At this point, a campaign is waged on the interior of the defined Gypsy, with the object of normalization. This is the current function of the site. It imposes a discipline on its inhabitants, and this is put on show for others as the consequence of moving outside the housing norm.

Foucault's analysis (1977) describes the disciplinary ethos of the workshop as facilitating capitalist production. The disciplinarization of a work force was the means of transforming laborers into labor power; thus, economic considerations merged with the aims of subjection and control. Production became dependent on control that was founded on knowledge of the worker and their work: the breaking down of tasks necessary to production into absolutely controllable units of work. This allowed the closest scrutiny. In effect, this production of labor power leads Foucault to conclude that "power produces reality," in that "it produces domains and objects of truth" (Foucault 1977, 194). The prison and the site are areas that fulfill the same ends, a production of reality, through a defined truth. They are both a means to an end; promoting a regime of normality within society—conformity to the needs of capitalism. In a similar way to the factory, in the jail each action of the prisoner is reduced to its most precise elements, so observation may be total and thus control maximized. Research into life on the site can be understood to function toward the same ends. The prison complemented the factory by acclimatizing the deviant to the regime of production, while the workplace informed the prison in the disciplinary strategies. Likewise, the site can be seen in the same way; it is in effect an area of punishment, either through poor conditions (relative to conventional housing) or through the control systems focused on the illegal site.

For Foucault, no individuated person is free from the process he describes; all are normalized to a greater or lesser extent. No one operates outside of the institutions of the disciplinary society. This landscape is Foucault's carceral—an apparatus of control based on an integratory and reintegratory force directed and informed by the knowledge it extracts. The prison is the most obvious aspect of this landscape; as such, it can be perceived as a crystallization of this whole environment that grows by implosion of power-knowledge; but the site can be understood as one of its progeny.

Power Relations

Foucault (1977) can be seen to be illuminating power relations with two distinct hues, one at the level of the body, the individual, the other referring to a whole politicophilosophical, sociohistoric spectrum. This book has undertaken something of the same exercise with regard to the Gypsy.

Placing the site in a cavalcade of power-relations, as one application of power within the great economy of power, we can argue that it is part of the expansive logic of the prison that spreads throughout the social field. The site, with no relation to nomadic existence, as a place of intransience or semipermanence, like the prison, has a social meaning beyond the position of Gypsies. The site tells us something about the nature of our society. The Gypsies are the focus of law because they breach the means of establishing market norms, mostly in housing and employment. The whole history of Gypsies can thus be seen to be enveloped in Foucault's carceral; the site is another application in the economy of power.

For Foucault, from the seventeenth century onwards, a new economy of power was necessary to the social form in which crime against property had become the principal transgression in the capitalist economy of illegalities. Contemporaneously, what legislation affecting Gypsies has addressed is part of a particular economy of illegalities, this legislation being in essence framed around principles of property. Out of this bourgeois economy of power emerges the power tactic of penal reform. For Foucault, the whole end of this movement, which arose alongside the prison, was the carrying through of the bourgeois economy, albeit by ostensibly humanitarian means. It was an attempt to make punishment more efficient while removing what would have become a mode of punishment dangerous to the new social form (emerging capitalism). The provision of sites is heralded as a humanitarian response, but it is the place where the unnameable, in terms of the housing market, are to be placed. When the Gypsy has been located on the site, a type of reform has been enacted. Taxes and rent can be extracted from named individuals who fall into a category: Gypsy.

The Individual Equals Punishment Equals Abstraction

Foucault (1977) illustrates the percolation of the carceral environment, creating an atmosphere of reciprocal institutions that at first informed the prison and then became informed by it. The range might include the school, the mad-house, the hospital, the site, and so on. This matrix of power-knowledge is the basis of Foucault's genealogy. As the criminal is created, so the lunatic, the student, the youth, the Gypsy are produced, all controllable according to their individuation, all objectified within this. Disciplinary society creates individuals and attaches these to definite populations.

As such, the ethnic category, arising out of social processes, becomes a focus of discipline. This can be understood to give rise to a similar response stimulated by other categories. For example, see figure 8.1.

Hence, the system reproduces itself. For Foucault, the individual is thus a constructed entity, through the techniques of power (established in the school, the prison, the site, etc.). This suggests that the development of the Gypsy population is connected to forms of social discipline. This analysis provides a social meaning of Gypsy ethnicity.

Foucault is attempting in his focus on the body to show how subjects are formed, how they are made objects of knowledge and regulated through this knowledge that is unique knowledge. Thus the Gypsy population is publicly defined as abnormal and is abstracted, placed on the periphery, its destiny being to reintegrate or be increasingly alienated. Some might see the self-confidence or assertiveness that has arisen among Gypsies because of this situation as a benefit, and maybe there are positive side effects. This is an area of weakness in Foucault's analysis in which he shows the tendency to deny individuals the chance to reassess human agency and intentions through self-confidence and resistance. However, as argued previously, solidarity can act to identify and solidify type or category in a negative way (Okely 1983, 77).

Foucault describes prison as having a contemporary function in the production of a delinquent milieu useful to the ruling class for the management of delinquency (Foucault 1977, 208). Here the site can again be seen as an extension of the prison, which operates to manage housing delinquency. According to Foucault, prison manages illegality; it does not repress or overcome it. The site has similar limitations. In contemporary society prison is, to a great extent, the depository of the prostitute, the shoplifter, and the traffic and drug offender. The site is the

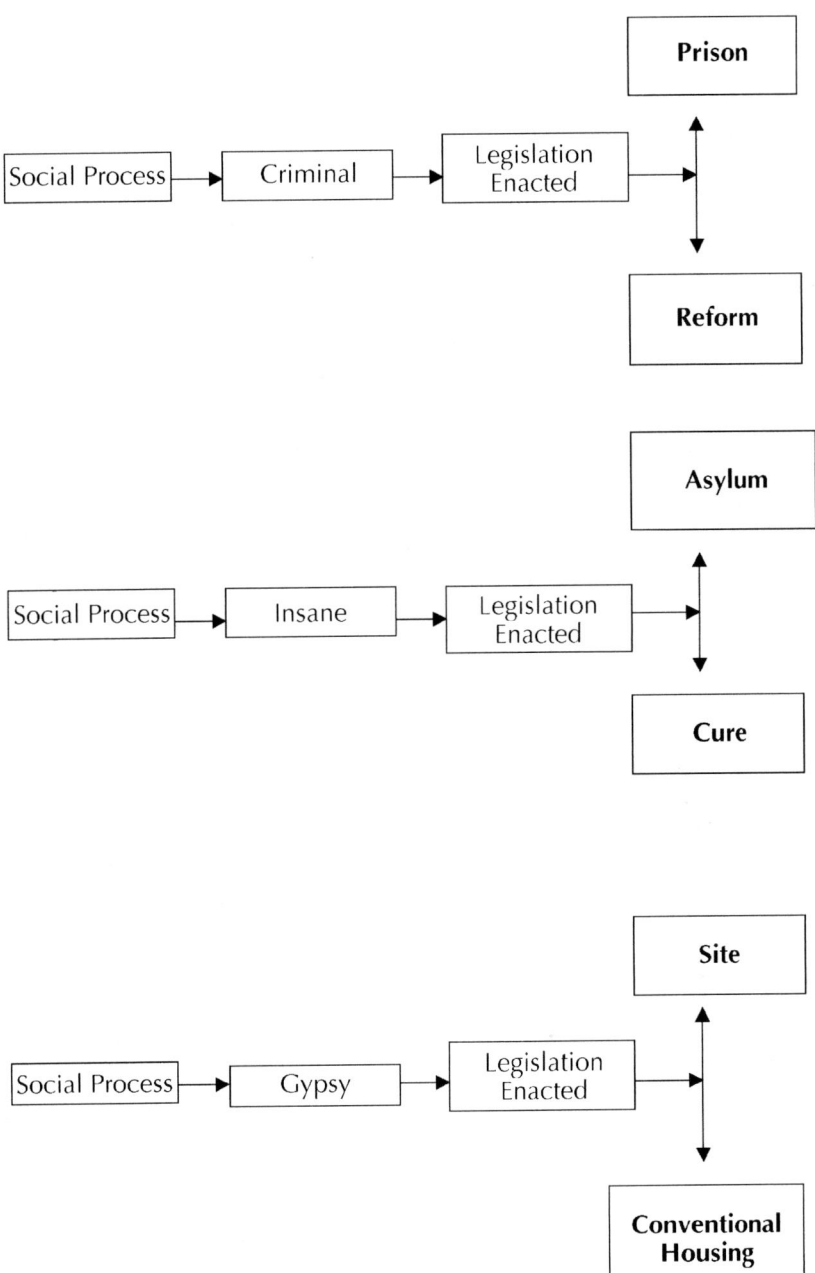

Figure 8.1. The Process of Categorization

assigned dwelling place of the Gypsy, he or she who is unwilling or unable to conform to the norms of housing discipline. The school, the workplace, the necessity to fit an acceptable mode of behavior for success, or even the least personal or familial security are the appliances used to control the potential for political activity that threatens market norms. But the prison today is not reform, it is not cure, and it is not management. It is possible that prison is not even essentially punishment, although it may have been at given periods in the past. The prison is now something other, where the other is assigned—it is a dumping ground for the unnameable. Yet again, in terms of housing the unnameable who have rejected or been ejected from conventional resorts, the site has a similar function to the prison.

For Foucault, power is not to be found in the amorphous state; hence, the analysis offered by Hawes and Perez (1995), who see Gypsies as the victims of the state, would be, for Foucault, fundamentally flawed. The technology of power, for Foucault, is dispersed throughout the social body. The state actually exists on the foundation of this diffusely exercised discipline—places such as the site, the designated location for the categorized group named Gypsies.

Breaking Away

Moving outside of the power nexus is not impossible. However, the removal of self is fraught with potential angst and confusion. I no longer see or feel myself to be a blood Gypsy. Because I do not live in a caravan, or ascribe to a Gypsy way of life, I have been told by career Gypsies that I am not a Gypsy. Yet the psychic stasis of these definers says much more about their spiritual, emotional, and intellectual incongruity relative to the identity they adhere to than all the words I have written in this book. I am proposing movement; they are settled. For all this, the further I move away from the idea of Gypsy roots the more I become categorized as non-Gypsy; I move or am moved from one ethnic chamber to another—another example of Foucault's ubiquitous carceral, the web of control within which we are all defined and wherein we are obliged to define ourselves and others.

Conclusion

In this chapter, I have, deploying Marxist and Foucauldian theory, suggested that legislation impacting on Gypsies is congruent with a social formation that will in its workings eliminate or reform structures and activities that fail to conform to the market norms on which it is premised. Within this argument, I have employed a Foucauldian genealogical analysis that defines the Gypsy as a product of power relations. I argue that the Gypsy has been created as a deviant and consigned to a place of control. As such, the legislation surrounding Gypsy lifestyles and the site can be understood as a mechanism of discipline complementary to and confirming of capitalist society. Lastly, I have argued that categorization is unavoidable; the moment I show I am not this or cease to hold fast to the facets of a particular label, I become (am made) part of some other category; the system perpetuates the violence of branding, and we are known by our marks.

9

Toward a New Paradigm of Gypsy Identity

In this book, I have argued that it is likely that what is recognized as the Gypsy population is in fact the product of very diverse social origins, without a specific ethnic root. This implies that the so-called Gypsy population needs to be thought of and responded to as a wide-ranging group of people, with differing social and cultural backgrounds and individual needs.

Overall, I have sought to heighten the awareness of the relationship between social phenomena in the generation of the Gypsy population and in doing so to question the idea of an essentialist and homogenous Gypsy population (the Gypsy ethnic narrative). It could be argued that the omission of this kind of analysis (the Gypsy population being portrayed as the product of ancestry, tradition, culture, and genetics) from the literature plays an important part in the development of the position that places Gypsies outside of society. As Goldberg has pointed out:

> *Race inscribes and circumscribes the experience of space and time, of geography and history, just as race itself acquires its specificity in terms of space-time correlates.* (1993, 206)

This discriminatory and stereotypical approach leads to an emphasis on particular types of response to and treatment of groups categorized as Gypsies.

A central concern of this book has been to highlight the role of social and economic forces in the generation of ethnicity in general and the narrative of Gypsy ethnicity in particular. As O'Connell argues,

> *Ethnicity is something which is produced in historically specific contexts, and it emerges, changes, and adapts in meaning over time.* (1994, 111–12)

The conceptual framework of the book proposes that forces other than biology and tradition have shaped what we perceive to be the Gypsy population. Throughout the book, the position that in effect argues for Gypsy ethnicity based on biological reductionism has been exposed. The literature concerned with Gypsy identity, while conceding that the Gypsy population has consistently recruited numbers of people from the settled community, has, with a few recent exceptions (Willems 1997; Lucassen et al. 1998) claimed that Gypsies have preserved a blood-line (O'Nions 1995, 13) and/or maintained themselves as a distinctive cultural group. From this background, the analysis of the Gypsy population presented in this book considers a range of issues, including the efficacy of notions of ethnic difference and the social purpose and meaning of the existence of the taxonomy of ethnic types.

The development of a perspective of Gypsy existence that exposes the role of social generation in the creation of such categories has broader connotations. The whole notion of ethnicity and some of the basic tenets of this realm of anthropology are brought into question. However, elaboration of this would have exceeded the aims of the book. Instead, it was more practical to consider Gypsies in a broader framework when looking at Gypsy identity, taking into account the type of insight shown by A. and F. Rehfisch when studying Scottish Travelers:

> *Literally gallons of ink have been utilized developing theories as to the origin of these people. It would seem to me to be an exercise in futility to review all of these and even more to attempt to justify any of them. Their origin is lost in the far past and can hardly be recon-*

> structed. For many centuries references exist mentioning the presence of nomadic bands wandering through the length and breadth of Scotland and occupying the economic niche, to a greater or lesser degree, that Travelers do today. (1975, 272)

Barth also offers a more cautious way forward from his research relating to Taters (a Gypsy-like people) in Norway:

> Taters thus form a despised group of very low economic standing—are indeed, a typical pariah section of the population. As such, the problem arises whether they constitute a true organized group within the larger Norwegian society, or whether the term Tater is merely a general label for a despised rural social status; sociologically comparable to "criminal" or "poor man." This problem is discussed by Heymowski who points out the several, partly contradictory criteria for the ascription of individuals to the group—descent, mode of life, physical appearance—and draws attention to the great fluctuations between different census accounts in the estimated number of Taters; based on ascription. (1975, 286)

Fascist Echoes

This seems to counter a disturbing undercurrent within the literature, the effort made to propose a definite, pure group being sustained over hundreds of years. The interpretation of Gypsy ethnicity, as traditionally understood and portrayed in the literature, might tell us more about the individual writers and their personalities, as well as their social and political context, than it does about Gypsies. Willems (1997) critically shows this to be the case with regard to what has become the accepted paradigm of Gypsy identity. This striving to present a unified whole, an identifiable grouping that may be categorized as a type, harks back to authoritarian Fascist regimes. Although the broad analysis of Gypsy identity is couched in terms of antiracism and political correctness, it seeks to differentiate people in terms of a typology based on custom, tradition, ethnicity, or race; it also proposes that this group belongs in certain situations (on sites/encampments or in trailers) or at least should be put together as a separate grouping). This seems an inherently racist analysis. The promotion of a nonsocial, noncontextual perspective, a Gypsy ethnic narrative, serves to heighten the ethical, moral, and analytical flaws in the literature. However, this perspective has other implications. Setting the position of Gypsies within a discourse of ethnicity and race, with a focus on discrimination, racism, and oppression, that turns non-Gypsies into the pariah group (the oppressors—see O'Nions 1995), does not adequately explain a possible relationship between the Gypsy population and the rest of society. This is because the writing on Gypsies tends to be highly emotive, set in romanticism, promoting a subjective analysis based on notions of individual and group psychology. It does not allow for the possible effects of phenomena, explored in this book, like social action (Kasler 1988, 150), social closure (Parkin 1979), narrative, or the dynamics of disciplinary society that move inextricably towards social norms that complement and confirm the character of the social formation by means of social control and punishment (Foucault 1977). Therefore, the analysis of the situation and nature of the Gypsy population, as contained in the literature, is partial.

In this vein, I have examined the disturbing, underlying or unconscious, set of attitudes that seem to be operating within the research surrounding Gypsies. This is, to some extent, demonstrated by Okely (1994, 20) when she uses Sartre's *Reflexions sur la question juive* as part of her attack on what she calls "non-ethnic, 'universalistic' categories" (1994, 19):

> There may not be so much difference between the anti-Semite and the democrat. The former wishes to destroy him as a man and leave nothing in him but the Jew, the pariah, the untouchable; the latter wishes to destroy him as a Jew and leave nothing in him but the man, the abstract and universal subject of the rights of man. (Sartre 1973, 57)

For Sartre, the ethnic or racial category is at least as important as all other considerations that define personhood. The sum of individual humanity is equated with type; he clearly states that type is the essence of humanity. He does not consider that we are made up of all sorts of other considerations that make us unique individuals. We are not separated from being the abstract and universal subject merely by ethnic or racial distinctions. In taking this position, Sartre is not far from the doctrine of the political right in seeing one's racial or ethnic type as decisive. In one way or another, most writers concerning themselves with Gypsies show some level of affiliation with this perspective.

Other Ways of Seeing

Anderson (1923), however, when writing about the American hobo, argues:

> *The irregularity of his employment is reflected in the irregularity of all phases of his existence. To deal with him as an individual, society must deal also with the economic forces which have formed his behavior, with the seasonal and cyclical fluctuations in industry.* (121)

For Anderson, the hobo type arose out of the social situation. Berthoff (1971) describes how hobos and tramps became more numerous in the United States during the economic crisis of the late nineteenth century when unemployment soared. These wanderers came to be classed with the unemployed as a dangerous group. Berthoff argues that as such their existence was connected to immigration and mobility within the United States that were themselves motivated by poverty and unemployment; in short, the dynamic movement of a laboring class in a time of mass industrialization (331). According to Thomas (1971), in becoming an American the immigrant was obliged to undertake "a suppression and repudiation of all the signs that distinguish him from us" (283). Those unable to make that adjustment were seen as holding on to dangerous characteristics that marked them out as different. Those who could or would not adapt were seen as a threat to the industrial state (Katzman and Tuttle 1982). Out of this process arose forms of castigation and discipline to comply with the norms of American society of the time. Gypsies in contemporary society might be understood to arise out of and exist in the same type of situation. This perspective would not support a universalistic, nonethnic outlook; the aim is not to destroy the Gypsy.

Questioning Ethnicity and Developing Identity

It is my contention that any system that promotes or idealizes ethnicity as a social category needs to be questioned. But I have shown that as a society we have a propensity to create ethnic narratives, and these can be understood as a means of creating meaning, a way of integrating ourselves and our activity into the otherwise chaotic maelstrom of life. However, J. Nicholas Entrikin states:

> *Narrative understanding has been characterized as a way of "seeing things together." It has been described as a distinct form of knowing that derives from the redescription of experience in terms of a synthesis of heterogeneous phenomena.* (1991, 23)

As Stuart Hall has more straightforwardly put it, "cultural identity is a matter of 'becoming' as well as being" (1990, 222–37). Entrikin points out that the narrative is a melding of incident and the account of the same that is mediated subjectively; they are never value free:

> *The narrative has two components, the story and the storyteller. Narratives are by definition told from the point of view of a subject or subjects.* (1991, 23–24)

However,

> *In narrative, events are given meaning through their configuration into a whole.* (24)

Gypsy identity will fit the series of narratives within which it takes its place. Thus, the origin and lifestyle of Gypsies as described, for example, by Heinrich Moritz Gottlieb Grellmann in the eighteenth century or George Borrow in the nineteenth century, as Willems (1997) illustrates, were generated within particular social configurations. A number of writers have noted the inherent contradictions in these stories about Gypsy origins. Okely states:

> It is not at all clear whether these so-called foreign Egyptians ever came from abroad. In 1562 the death penalty was introduced for those "calling themselves *Egyptians*" (my emphasis) *and for those "counterfeiting, transforming or disguising themselves in their Apparel, Speech or other behaviour" (Thompson 1928). This suggests that the Egyptian title was nothing but an assumed identity for many persons with no foreign origin. It may have been a convenient means of self-identification among Gypsies in order to present an exotic identity as fortune-tellers and dancers. Further evidence reveals a description of a hundred Gypsies in the early seventeenth century who went about "causing their face to be made blacke, as if they were Egyptians" (Thompson 1928: 34). Thus the popular view that all the early Gypsies were innately different in physiognomy or so-called "racial origin" should be treated with scepticism.* (1994, 7–8)

As Willems demonstrates (1997, 171–95), these archaic interpretations remain the basis of the current analysis of Gypsy identity. It is this ossification of analysis that this book has sought to address. I suggest that the existing narrative of Gypsy identity is partial; to an extent it is uninformed by the social configuration within which it is constructed and maintained. The effect of this is that the narrative of Gypsy identity moves exponentially further away from the social configuration of which it is a part, becoming more self-contradictory and less useful as an explanatory tool. This is what Kuhn (1963) described as a paradigm in crisis or what Prigogine (1980) might characterize as the progress of a dissipating structure.

In order that the narrative of Gypsy identity become more useful, it must be formed within and out of the social context of which it is a part; it needs to be informed by contemporary social, economic, and political considerations and conditions. The claims of the writers involved in establishing the nature of Gypsy identity are hardly placed in context at any point, as Okely demonstrates:

> *It was not until the late eighteenth and early nineteenth centuries that scholars and linguists claimed an Indian origin for Gypsies, on the basis of various forms of Romany "language," dialects or vocabulary. In the folklorist and other literature the claim is that the "real" Gypsies are found in England and Wales but not in Ireland and Scotland. The*

> *fact that the first "Egyptian" was recorded in Scotland is strangely overlooked. Yet the presences of "Egyptians" in Scotland was not just a one-off record in 1505. Again in 1530 "Egyptians" danced for James V in Holyrood House, Edinburgh, and were rewarded for their entertainment.* (1994, 8)

This propensity hides the means and context of Gypsy culture and how the population has developed through social and economic factors. The effort to establish exotic origin obfuscates similarities between itinerant groups and between Gypsies and non-Gypsy communities:

> *I suggest that the sub-classification of Gypsies or Travelers in Britain and Ireland in terms of the presences of absence of exotic Indian Romany origins, has more to do with internal colonialism than with actual differences between groups. Gypsies or Travelers are both defined and sub-classified by the dominant society and by themselves. There are many aspects of Gypsy or Traveler culture which the different groups have in common, it is only the labels, the territorial and kinship allegiances, and local contexts for working and living which demarcate differences.* (Okely 1994)

The current analysis and narrative of Gypsy identity are founded on ideas formed within an era of liberal paternalism but also in a time of nationalist fervor and attempts to understand humankind through eugenic categorization (Willems 1997). This limits our comprehension of the malleability of Gypsy identity, but it also restricts our understanding of the nature of our social formation. While we subscribe to the teleological position that Gypsies just are because of vague blood desire, or natural propensity, we are blinded to rational, social, and economic explanations of the generation of the Gypsy population. The social and economic analysis and narrative of Gypsy identity expose the forms of discipline and control that are exerted on Gypsies in the interest of market norms and that oblige conformity to the same.

A Place for the Gypsies

This book has critically examined the contemporary narrative of Gypsy identity, which places ethnicity at the center of the explanation as to why Gypsies exist and persist. Considerations of tradition, hereditary, culture, and sentiment produce a notion that the site (encampment) is a desired community location in the collective Gypsy mind. The notion that Gypsies have a natural place and predetermined station in society runs through the literature and theory pertaining to this population. McDonagh exemplifies this. Although he states that nomadism is as much a state of mind as a state of fact (1994, 96), he goes on to argue that it is impossible to house Gypsies due to a kind of psychological neurosis to housing, and in effect demands a lower rung of housing provision by way of permanent and temporary sites (95–109).

However, the paradigm or narrative of Gypsy identity needs to accommodate the social and economic realities of living in an environment wherein housing supply is premised on income and the market. If these considerations are included in the narrative of Gypsy identity, it may become clear that the housing market is insufficient in terms of meeting society's housing requirements. This is perhaps the usefulness of the ethnic narrative of Gypsy identity in terms of state interest. The energy that fuels its persistence via the reactionary analysis that dominates the literature focusing on Gypsies may be the antisocial, market-led nature of our society.

Dangerous Categorization

Perhaps the most crucial aspect of this book is that it demonstrates that the academic response to Gypsy identity departs from the contemporary discourse on ethnicity. The writing on and about Gypsies has much more in common with older reductionist notions of race (see Montagu 1997). Appiah and Gutmann (1996, 164–66) point out the dangers associated with social categorization by ethnicity or race:

> *The very act of identifying with people of "one's own race" simply by virtue of their being of one's own race has had the psychological effect of undermining mutual identification among individual human beings. (Something similar can be said about some national and ethnic identifications). Absent our mutual identification, we are likely to be*

less motivated to ensure that justice is done for people who look and act differently from ourselves. Defying logic but catering to human weakness, racial identification has the capacity to rationalise injustice by a process of transference analogous to the one described by Frederick Douglass over a century ago:

"The evils most fostered by slavery and oppression are precisely those which slaveholders and oppressors would transfer for their system to the inherent character of their victims. Thus the very crimes of slavery become slavery's best defence. By making the enslaved a character fit only for slavery, they excuse themselves for refusing to make the slave a free man. A wholesale method of accomplishing this result is to overthrow the instinctive consciousness of the common brotherhood of man."

This book asks those seeking to establish or confirm the idea of a Gypsy ethnicity to consider the above. A brave student of the future might usefully research the social and psychological motivation of those who continue to resuscitate what is, in effect, a contention that a race or ethnicity of Gypsies exists in a concrete and definitive sense. This courageous pilgrim might hold in mind that it is too easy to cite the cause as being a shared desire on the part of theorists and writers to perpetuate a romantic, rural, middle-class idyll, although as Guy points out,

the Romantic stereotype of the Gypsy, as an exotic and noble primitive, wandering unconstrained as the mood takes him. (1975, 203)

has been cherished by members of an exploitative class who have had the leisure to fantasize about Gypsy freedom (203). It would also be unsatisfactory to interpret the volatile defense of Gypsies (Hawes and Perez 1995; Acton 1974) as a symptom of neocolonialist displacement and transference. However, the romantic, idealized admiration of Gypsies as a kind of roving antediluvian patrician race can be understood as a form of unconscious inverted racism. Guy (1975, 203) detects this propensity, citing Fanon to make the point:

To us, the man who adores the Negro is as "sick" as the man who abominates him. . . . In the absolute, the black is no more to be loved than the Czech, and truly what is to be done is to set man free. (Fanon 1952)

The consequences of a similar adoration of Gypsies have been noted by Okely:

The difference between Travelers and non-Travelers has been exaggerated and mythologised. Travelers or Gypsies have been accredited with exotic, romantic qualities. This exoticisation might appear harmless and aesthetically enriching when found in poetry, painting, opera and fiction, but the imagery lives on and may be used as a device to reject most if not all living Travelers and Gypsies. Once perceived as exotic beings, the circumstances are ripe for dividing dream from reality, phantom from person. (1994, 5)

It could be the case that the literature on Gypsies has developed its own cultural paradigm, complete with rites, rituals, and language, from which it may be difficult to depart—an ethnicity of Gypsiologists? However, the constant insistence on developing the notion of a Gypsy type based on hereditary ethnic considerations, biological blood transference, or inherited cultural traits (race by another name) seems to be part of an outdated anthropological debate. As Appiah and Gutmann point out,

The idea of pure races is a myth. Much of the story of the genetics of race—a field promoted by some of the most eminent scientists of their day—turns out to have been prejudice dressed up as science.... The moral issues raised by our own biology—racism, sexual stereotypes, and claims that selfishness, spites and nationalism are driven by genes—are just that: issues of ethics rather than science and that science has nothing to do with how we perceive or treat our fellow human beings. (1996, 262)

However, not only are notions of race and ethnicity vulnerable to the scrutiny of biological or genetic analysis, they have little common sense credibility. In the words of Sollars, "What were the givens in intellectual pursuits until recently have now become problematic issues"(1989, x).

Toward a New Paradigm of Gypsy Identity

It is clear from the material presented in this book that a different standpoint on Gypsy identity is required and that the whole emphasis on ethnicity relating to Gypsies needs to be reassessed. While the development of the kind of universalism suggested by Gilroy (2000, 327–58) might be too idealistic at the present time, given the impact of social and economic inequalities inherent in the current social formation (capitalism) as Gilroy (2000, 11–53, 97–134) suggests, contemporary society may have reached a moment wherein there is the opportunity to rid itself of the human taxonomies of race and ethnicity that have been shown as partial, flawed, and destructive. It seems, given our current and potential knowledge and awareness of the biological, psychological, and social makeup of humanity, that we need to develop a new paradigm about the way we think about ourselves and question if this needs to involve forms of categorization that are some way intrinsic to our being.

The analysis presented in this book allows Gypsies to begin to be situated within the general social context. It is an attempt, through the development of social understanding of Gypsies, to go beyond the vague notions, premised on mystery, subjectivity, romanticism, and near superstition that surround the study of this population. The book as a whole is arguing for a change in perspective in terms of establishing the character and nature of Gypsy identity. This does not merely demand a different emphasis. What is required is a movement away from an essentialist analysis premised on biological assumptions and romantic folklore traditions toward a commitment to a broader conceptual framework that is able to encompass wide social and economic considerations as crucial factors in the generation and categorization of populations. Given the inherent contradictions in the notion of Gypsy ethnicity exposed in this book, it is clear that a new paradigm of identity formation with regard to this group is needed.

This book has consistently argued that Gypsies should be understood as being a heterogeneous population, developing out of and reflecting the social and economic situation in which it exists.

This proposal does not disqualify hereditary or biological links between individuals and families within this group, but it questions these as necessary qualifications, or in the absence of blood ties, as limiting factors in terms of identity. In short, this perspective questions the Gypsy phenomenon as being necessarily a type, set in permanent, unchanging ethnicity, race, or history, and presents a new paradigm of Gypsies as a group of people responding to definite social, including family and institutional conditions and/or economic exigencies, choices, obligations, or pressures.

Genetic Corroboration

The need for an alternative perspective of Gypsy identity is confirmed by Kalaydjieva (1998). She examined the parallels between the social and genetic history of Gypsies through a large study of three independent Gypsy groups. According to her:

> *These three groups do not intermarry and have well defined and distinct group identity, yet all three share a rare gene mutation, suggesting at some point in their history these groups have shared a common gene pool.* (1998, 1)

She explained:

> *I thought of Gypsies in the ignorant way typical of most outsiders, that is a single population which is socially and genetically uniform. Gradually, I have come to realize that what we describe with the generic category of "Gypsies" is in fact a very complicated stratified hierarchical structure.* (1998, 1)

For Kalaydjieva, the basic unit of social organization within the Gypsy population is the Gypsy group, the identity of which is founded on historical migrations, trade, tradition, language, and in some instances "organs of self-rule" (1998, 1). However, she has concluded that

> *The overall structure is not static and has been described as fluid mosaic where splits and merges between different groups have occurred many times in history.* (1998, 1)

The study, which has involved leading geneticists and Gypsy ethnologists from all over the world, is now focused on finding the split in the common genetic origin of Gypsies. However, according to Kalaydjieva:

> *The most amazing finding is the extent to which they have diverged genetically—these three Gypsy groups are at present more different to each other than the classical outlier populations of Europe (the Finns the Basques and the Sardinians) which no geneticist would dream of pooling together. This despite of the fact that they live in close proximity to each other, sometimes in the same villages, and is obviously based on differences in culture and tradition of whose existence we are totally ignorant.* (1998, 2)

For Kalaydjieva, these findings are relevant in terms of future genetic research insofar as they indicate that

> *important differences may and do exist between Gypsy groups and that pooling patients from different groups together may have a strong confounding effect.* (1998, 2)

This analysis, which has been developed and broadened (Kalaydjieva, Gresham, and Calafell 2001), demonstrates that the idea of a homogenous Gypsy ethnic identity has little biological basis. This contradicts the characteristic academic perspective. For example, according to Okely:

> *No one could simply take to the road and become a Traveler—he or she could gain some acceptance through marriage, but only the offspring could claim full ethnic identity.* (1984, 9)

and

> *A person has to have at least one Traveler or Gypsy parent to claim membership. The children of a mixed marriage between Traveller and gorgio . . . can claim rights of membership through descent.* (1984, 9)

However, Kalaydjieva's findings suggest, in a quite concrete way, that Gypsy ethnicity is essentially a social construction. This represents a serious biologically based challenge to the idea of a homogenous Gypsy identity founded on hereditary or biological factors. The latter analysis is favored by the academic discourse relating to Gypsies as the foundation on which other forms of ethnic attachments are premised. These include sentiment; vague political standpoints; the consequences of ambitions of state power, as exemplified in legislation (see chapter 5); and obscure folk mythologies (Willems 1997).

Hope in Crisis

The establishing of identity, with its incumbent process of exclusion and inclusion (see Shields 1992; Maffesoli 1996; Munro 1998), is important to the modern individual who appears to be constantly involved in instituting, reiterating, reviewing, and reestablishing his or her self-identity. This might be understood as what has become known in contemporary society as the identity crisis (see Wirth 1964; Schmalenbach 1977; 1980; Maffesoli 1996). But this gives hope for the more flexible interpretation of identity proposed at the start of this section. As Hetherington (2000, 92–93) has pointed out, we now choose groups rather than identify with primary groups like the family. This model has been consistently fascinating to sociologists (for example, Maffesoli 1996) as has the idea of the impact of consumer society (Bauman 1990, 1991; Maffesoli 1988, 1996) that undermines traditional social roles associated with, for example, the family through reference to mass influences wherein an individualization takes place. In the face of this, people are obliged to become part of what Hetherington has described as neo-tribes and elective communities (2000, 93).

As might be expected of sociological analysis, these positions see social change as the motivator of identity formation; the family, kinship, and community pressures, what might be called traditional generators of identity, are seen to be shrinking in significance in terms of their effect on identity formation.

This would seem to undermine the notion of Gypsy ethnicity as portrayed in the literature that places primary groups at the center of ethnic construction. However, as this book has shown, in terms of Gypsy identity, the traditional mechanisms of identity are at work alongside social and economic influences, and it might be argued that it is this combination of effects that gives rise to Gypsy ethnicity and its accompanying narrative. This book has argued that this amalgamation of social and economic phenomena arises out of the social formation (the political environment) and as such would be seen by Weber as having the capacity to motivate the development of ethnic identity:

> *Ethnic membership does not constitute a group; it only facilitates group formation of any kind, particularly in the political sphere. On the other hand, it is primarily the political community, no matter how artificially organized, that inspires the belief in common ethnicity.* (Weber 1922, 389)

Perhaps the greatest obstacle to the development of a new paradigm of Gypsy identity is the apparent inability of theorists and those involved in Gypsy issues to make this connection.

Compounding Difference

The notion of ethnicity was only widely deployed when the concept of race became unpalatable. It replaced the biological, blood, and hereditary distinctions of race with differentiation based on custom and tradition. But in practice the ideas of race and ethnicity have melded in popular contemporary discourse. There is no difference between the practices of ethnic cleansing and racial extermination, for example. In contemporary usage what we call ethnicity constitutes a much more complex formation of traits and characteristics than a coalescing within the political sphere. What we are talking about in everyday discourse and in the literature concentrating on ethnicity is compound difference. This is more of a defining mechanism than race. It has the power to mark out ethnic types based on any factor of difference. This does not help with the kind of problem presented by Ashley Montagu:

> *The idea of "race" represents one of the most dangerous myths of our time, and one of the most tragic. . . . Race is the witchcraft, the de-*

monology of our time, the means by which we exorcise imagined demoniacal powers among us. (1997, 41)

Although Montagu goes on to offer the ethnic group as a more palatable alternative to the idea of race, on the strength of this term's original usage and interpretation (186), ethnicity, like culture, in a period where the expression and practice of ethnic cleansing has been used to denote the persecution or murder of groups that can be identified as different, as the other is a problematic concept.

The dangers involved in the concept of racial difference do not need further elaboration here; Montagu makes a good enough job of this, so including such an exercise in this present work would be no more than reiteration. However, John Stuart Mill makes a strikingly original and relatively contemporary point:

> *I have long felt that the prevailing tendency to regard all the marked distinctions of human character as innate, and in the main indelible, and ignore the irresistible proofs that by far the greater part of those differences, whether between individuals, races, or sexes, are such as not only might but naturally would be produced by differences in circumstances, is one of the chief hindrances to the rational treatment of great social questions, and one of the greatest stumbling blocks to the human improvement.* (J. S. Mill, *Autobiography* [1873], quoted in Montagu 1997, 44)

This seems to be the fundamental problem about conflating differences, be they innate as in the concept of race or ethnicity, or indelible, in terms of tradition, rite, ritual, and culture, with situations, events, or issues that are profoundly intertwined with social forces and the character of the social formation. There has been little time or space given to the kind argument put forward by Mill, that the behavior of Gypsies is "such as not only might but naturally would be produced by differences in circumstances." The myth, as Montagu would have it, can prevent appropriate action.

The arguments made in this book clearly indicate that the exercise of seeking to identify differences is something of an outmoded pursuit. Clifford suggests,

> It is increasingly clear . . . that the concrete activity of representing a culture, subculture, or indeed any coherent domain of collective activity is always strategic and selective. The world's societies are too systematically interconnected to permit any easy isolation of separate or independently functioning systems. The increased pace of historical change . . . forces a new self-consciousness about the way cultural wholes and boundaries are constructed and translated. . . . What is hybrid or "historical" in an emergent sense has been less commonly collected and presented as a system of authenticity. (1988, 231)

Given this, and the possible dire consequences of ethnic distinction, one wonders if the whole project of ethnic categorization has outlived its usefulness as a successor to the damaging categorization of race. Ethnicity does seem to be spiraling into the same problems of contradiction in use and confusion of definition that marked the demise of its theoretical predecessor. If indeed ethnicity has its roots and force in social change, why do we need to align with it anymore? If the Gypsy population is a product of social conditions and interactions, would it not be more accurate and productive to admit that the phenomena involved are the generators of the crucial factors in human distinction and the resulting inequalities rather than seek to make marginal and fragile hereditary and biological boundaries the pivot of perceived differences?

Appendix: The Gypsy Lore Society (GLS)

The GLS was founded in 1888 by a number of non-Travelers (whose interest had in large measure been aroused by the writings of George Borrow: see Willems 1997, *George Borrow (1803–81): The Walking Lord of Gypsy Lore*, 93–170).

The GLS had a short initial history, collapsing in on itself in 1892. However, it was revived in 1907 and survived with a few intermissions up to present times.

At first, contemporary political issues received scant attention in the pages of the *Journal of the Gypsy Lore Society*. Having managed to attract to its ranks most of the authorities in Europe and North America on Gypsy lore and language, the primary objective of the GLS became the gathering together of scholarly material. However, in 1908, responding to political pressure to pass a Movable Dwellings Bill, the GLS began to attempt to influence opinion about and the treatment of Gypsies (Fraser 1992, 256). Since 1989, it has been headquartered in the United States.

In the modern period, the GLS saw itself as an international association of persons interested in Gypsy and Traveler studies. Its goals include promotion of the study of Gypsy, Traveler, and analogous peripatetic cultures worldwide; dissemination of accurate information aimed at increasing understanding of these cultures in their diverse forms; and establishment of closer contacts among scholars studying any aspects of these cultures.

The Gypsy collections at the University of Liverpool hold the GLS Archive and the Scott Macfie Gypsy Collection (this is a collection of materials of special interest to Gypsy historians). The Gypsy collections include books, manuscripts, prints, photographs, sound recordings, and press cuttings and are a major resource for Gypsy and Romany studies.

The main historical focus of the collections is the period from the mid-nineteenth to the mid-twentieth centuries. Material from the collections can be viewed at: sca.lib.liv.ac.uk/collections/gypsy/intro.htm.

In 2000, the *Journal of the Gypsy Lore Society* became *Romani Studies*. Under the sponsorship of the GLS (formerly Gypsy Lore Society, North American Chapter), *Romani Studies* features articles on the cultures of groups traditionally known as Gypsies as well as Travelers and other peripatetic groups. These groups include, among others, those referring to themselves as Ludar, Rom, Roma, Romanichels, Sinti, and Travelers. The journal publishes articles in history, anthropology, sociology, linguistics, art, literature, folklore, and music, as well as reviews of books and audiovisual materials.

Bibliography

Acton, T. (1974) *Gypsy Politics and Social Change.* London: Routledge and Kegan Paul Ltd.
Adams, B., Okely, J. M., Morgan, D., and Smith, D. (1975) *Gypsies and Government Policy in England.* London: Heinemann.
Anderson, N. (1923) *The Hobo: The Sociology of the Homeless Man.* Chicago: University of Chicago Press.
Anon. (1835) *Memorabilia of the City of Glasgow.* Glasgow.
Appiah, K. A. and Gutmann, A. (1996) *Color Conscious.* Princeton, New Jersey: Princeton University Press.
Axon, W. (1897) "Laws Relating to Gypsies," in Andrews, W. (ed.). *Legal Lore: Curiosities of Law and Lawyers,* 165–78. London, Andrews and Co.
Banton, M. (1987) *Racial Theories.* Cambridge: Cambridge University Press.
Barth, F. (1969) *Introduction to Ethnic Groups and Boundaries.* St. Albans, Hertfordshire: Allen and Unwin Ltd.
———. (1970) *Ethnic Groups and Boundaries.* London: George Allen and Unwin.
———. (1975) "The Social Organization of a Pariah Group in Norway," in Rehfisch, F. (ed.). *Gypsies, Tinkers and Other Travellers,* 285–99. London: Academic Press Inc., Ltd.
Bauman, Z. (1990) "Effacing the Face: On the Social Management of Moral Proximity." *Theory, Culture and Society* 7 (1): 5–38.
Beier, A. L. (1985) *Masterless Men: The Vagrancy Problem in England, 1560–1640.* London and New York: Methuen.

Belton, B. A. (2004) *Gypsy and Traveller Ethnicity: The Social Generation of an Ethnic Phenomenon.* London: Routledge.
Benton, B. (1985) *Ellis Island: A Pictorial History.* New York: Facts on File Publications.
Berthoff, R. (1971) *An Unsettled People: Social Order and Disorder in American History.* New York: Harper and Row.
Biko, S. (1986) *I Write What I Like.* London: Heinemann.
Boas, F. (1911) *The Mind of Primitive Man.* New York: Free Press.
Brecht, B. (1985) *Mother Courage and Her Children.* London: Methuen.
Brewer, A. (1984) *A Guide to Marx's Capital.* Cambridge: Cambridge University Press.
Brown, I. (1924) *Gypsy Fires in America.* New York: Harper & Brothers.
Bruner, J. (1987) "Life as Narrative." *Social Research* 54 (1): 11–32.
Burnett, S. M. (1889) "A Note on the Melungeons." *American Anthropologist*, October, 347–49.
Butchart, A. (1998) *The Anatomy of Power: European Constructions of the African Body.* London: Zed Books Ltd.
Carver, T. (1982) *Marx's Social Theory.* Oxford: Oxford University Press.
Chambers, R. (1858) *Domestic Annals of Scotland from the Reformation to the Revolution.* Vol. II. Edinburgh: Chambers.
Clebert, J. P. (1963) *The Gypsies.* London: Readers Union Ltd.
Clifford, J. (1988) *The Predicament of Culture.* Massachusetts: Harvard University Press.
Coelho, A. (1892). *Os Ciganos de Portugal, com um estudo sobre o Calão.* Lisbon: National Printing Office.
Crabb, J. (1831) *The Gipsies' Advocate.* London: Seeley and Co.
De Man, P. (1984) *The Rhetoric of Romanticism.* New York: Columbia University Press.
Dublin Travellers Education and Development Group. (1992) *Traveller Ways Traveller Words.* Dublin: Pavee Point Publications.
Dunn, R. S. (1962) "The Barbados Census of 1680." *Journal of the Barbados Museum and Historical Society* 33 (2): 57–75.
Durkheim, E. (1915) *Elementary Forms of Religious Life.* St. Albans, Hertfordshire: Allen and Unwin Ltd.
Earle, F., Dearling, A., Whittle, H., Glasse, R., and Gubby. (1994) *A Time to Travel.* Dorset: Enabler Publications.
Encarta Online. (1998) "Social Science: Anthropology Roma" in *Encarta Concise Encyclopaedia.* Encarta Online.

Entrikin, J. Nicholas. (1991) *The Betweenness of Place*. Baltimore: Johns Hopkins University Press.
Fanon, F. (1965) *The Wretched of the Earth*. Harmondsworth: Macgibbon and Kee/Penguin Books Ltd.
———. (1967) *Black Skins, White Masks*. London: Pluto Press.
Flew, A. (2002) *A Dictionary of Philosophy*. London: Pan Books Ltd.
Fonseca, I. (1995) *Bury Me Standing*. London: Chatto and Windus.
Foucault, M. (1972) *The Archaeology of Knowledge*. London: Tavistock Publications Ltd.
———. (1977) *Discipline and Punish*. Harmondsworth: Penguin Books Ltd.
———. (1986) "Nietzsche, Genealogy, History," in Rabinow, P., (ed.). *The Foucault Reader*, 83–89. London: Peregrine.
Fraser, A. (1992) *The Gypsies*. Oxford and Massachusetts: Blackwell Publishers Ltd.
Geana, G. (1997) "Ethnicity and Globalization: Outline of a Complementarist Conceptualization." *Social Anthropology* 5 (2): 197–209.
Gilroy, P. (2000) *Between Camps: Race, Identity, and Nationalism at the End of the Colour Line*. London: Allen Lane The Penguin Press.
Goffman, E. (1959) *The Presentation of Self in Everyday Life*. Harmondsworth: Penguin Books Ltd.
Goldberg, D. T. (1993) *Racist Culture*. Massachusetts and Oxford: Blackwell Publishers.
Goldschmidt, W. (1990) *The Human Career: The Self in the Symbolic World*. Oxford: Blackwell Publishers.
Gordon, C., ed. (1980) *Power/Knowledge: Selected Interviews and Other Writings 1972–1977 by Michael Foucault*. New York: Pantheon.
Gropper, R. C. (1975) *Gypsies in the City*. Princeton, New Jersey: Darwin Press.
Guttman, A. (1978) *Gambling and Gamblers*. New York: Columbia University Press.
Guy, W. (1975) "Ways of Looking at Roms: The Case of Czechoslovakia," in Rehfisch, F., (ed.). *Gypsies, Tinkers, and Other Travellers*, 202–23. London: Academic Press Inc., Ltd.
Hall, G. (1915) *The Gipsy's Parson*. London: Low, Marston and Co.
Hall, S. (1990) "Cultural Identity and Diaspora," in Rutherford, J., (ed.). *Identity, Community, Culture, and Difference*, 222–37. London: Lawrence and Wishart Ltd. First published in *Framework* 1 (36).
———. (1991) "The Local and the Global," in King, A. D., (ed.). *Culture, Globalisation, and the World System* 19–39. London: Macmillan.

———. (1994) "Cultural Identity and Diaspora," in Williams, P. and Chrisman, L. (eds.). *Colonial Discourse and Postcolonial Theory* 392–403. London: Routledge.

Hancock, I. (1980) "Gullah and Barbadian: Origins and Relationships." *American Speech* 55 (i): 17–35.

———. (1987) *The Pariah Syndrome: An Account of Gypsy Slavery and Persecution*. Ann Arbor: Karoma.

Hancock, I., Dowd, S., and Djuric, R., eds. (1998) *The Roads of the Roma*. Hertfordshire: University of Hertfordshire Press.

Handler, J. (1970) "The Amerindian Slave Population of Barbados in the Seventeenth and Early Eighteenth Centuries," *Journal of the Barbados Museum and Historical Society* 33 (3): 111–36.

Hawes, D., and Perez, B. (1995) *The Gypsy and the State*. Bristol: SAUS Publications.

Hetherington, K. (2000) *New Age Travellers: Vanloads of Uproarious Humanity*. London and New York: Cassell.

Hewitt, J. P. (1979) *Self and Society*. 2nd ed. Massachusetts: Allyn and Bacon.

Hoyland, J. (1816) *A Historical Survey of the Customs, Habits, and Present State of the Gypsies*. York: Hoyland.

Hyman, M. (1989) *Sites for Travellers*. London: Race and Housing Research Unit.

Jenkins, R. (1996) *Social Identity*. London: Routledge.

———. (1997) *Rethinking Ethnicity*. London: Sage Publications Ltd.

Jinadu A. L. (1986) *Fanon: In Search of the African Revolution*. London: KPI Limited.

Jones, S. (1993) *The Language of the Genes*. London: HarperCollins Publishers Ltd.

Journal of the Gypsy Lore Society (1892), 61.

Jusserand, J. (1988) *English Wayfaring Life in the Middle Ages*. Corner House Williamstown, MA, and London: repr. 1974 Methuen Books Ltd.

Kalaydjieva, L., et al. in *Univation, Gypsies, and Genetics: New Paths to Understanding* (July 1998). At: www.avcc.edu.au/avcc/pubs/univation/jul98/page9.htm.

Kalaydjieva, L., Gresham, G., and Calafell, F. (2001) *Genetic Studies of the Roma (Gypsies): A Review* (BMC Medical Genetics 2:5.1471–2350/2/5).

Kasler, D. (1988) *Max Weber*. Cambridge: Polity Press.

Katzman, D. M., and Tuttle, W. M., eds. (1982) *Plain Folk: The Life Stories of Undistinguished Americans*. Illinois: University of Illinois Press.

Kenrick, D., and Bakewell, S. (1990) *On the Verge: The Gypsies of England*. London: Runnymede Trust.

Kenrick, D., and Clark, C. (1995) *The Gypsies and Travellers of Britain*. Hatfield, Hertfordshire: University of Hertfordshire Press.

Kornblum, W. (1975) "Boyash Gypsies: Shantytown Ethnicity," in Rehfisch, F., (ed.). *Gypsies, Tinkers, and Other Travellers* 123–38. London: Academic Press Inc., Ltd.

Kuhn, F. (1963) "The Function of Dogma in Scientific Research in Scientific Change," in Crombie, A. C., (ed.). *Scientific Change: Historical Studies in the Intellectual, Social, and Technical Conditions for Scientific Discovery and Technical Invention, from Antiquity to the Present*, 347–69. London: Heinemann Publications.

Kuper, A. (1983) *Anthropology and Anthropologists: The Modern British School*. London: Routledge.

Kuper, L., and Smith, M. G., eds. (1971) *Pluralism in Africa*. Berkeley: University of California Press.

Lasch, C. (1980) *The Culture of Narcissism*. London: Abacus.

Lee, P. J. (2000) *We Borrow the Earth: An Intimate Portrait of the Gypsy Shamanic Tradition and Culture*. London: Thorsons.

Lee, W. (1999) *Dark Blood: A Romany Story*. London: Minerva.

Liegeois, J. P. (1985) *Gypsies and Travellers*. Strasbourg: Council of Europe Press.

———. (1986) *Gypsies: An Illustrated History*. London: Al Saqi Books.

———. (1994) *Roma, Gypsies, Travellers*. Strasbourg: Council of Europe Press.

Lockwood, W. G. and Salo, S. (1994) *Gypsies and Travelers in North America*.

Lucassen, J., Willems, W., and Cottaar, A. (1998) *Gypsies and Other Itinerant Groups: A Socio-Historical Approach*. Basingstoke, Hampshire: Macmillan Press Ltd.

MacRitchie, D. (1894) *Scottish Gypsies under the Stuarts*. Edinburgh: Constable.

McCann, M., O'Siochain, S., and Ruane, J. (1994) "Introduction," in McCann, M., O'Siochain, S., and Ruane, J., (eds.). *Irish Travellers: Culture and Ethnicity*, i–xiii. Belfast: Institute of Irish Studies, Queens University Belfast.

McCarthy, P. (1994) "The Sub-Culture of Poverty Reconsidered," in McCann, M., O'Siochain, S., and Ruane, J., (eds.). *Irish Travellers: Culture and Ethnicity*, 123–24. Belfast: Institute of Irish Studies, Queens University Belfast.

McDonagh, M. (1994) "Nomadism in Irish Travellers' Identity" in McCann, M., O'Siochain, S., and Ruane, J. (eds.) *Irish Travellers: Culture and Ethnicity,* 94–95. Belfast: Institute of Irish Studies, Queens University, Belfast.
McNay, L. (1994) *Foucault: A Critical Introduction.* Cambridge: Polity Press.
Maffesoli, M. (1988) "Jeux de masques: Postmodern Tribalism." *Design Issues* 4 (1–2): 141–51.
Maffesoli, M. (1996) *The Time of the Tribes.* London: Sage Publications.
Magee, B. (1987) *The Great Philosophers.* London: BBC Books.
Malik, K. (1996) *The Meaning of Race.* Basingstoke, Hampshire: Macmillan Press Ltd.
Mallory, J. P. (1989) *In Search of the Indo-Europeans: Language, Archaeology, and Myth.* London: Thames and Hudson.
Mandel, E. (1979) *Introduction to Marxist Economic Theory.* London: Pathfinder.
Marcuse, H. (1968) *Reason and Revolution.* Boston: Beacon Press.
Marx, K. (1887) *Capital.* Vol. 1. Moscow: Foreign Languages Publishing House (1961 ed.).
———. (1935) *The Eighteenth Brumaire of Louis Bonaparte.* New York: International Publishers.
Mayall, D. (1988) *Gypsy-Travellers in the Nineteenth-Century Society.* Cambridge: Cambridge University Press.
———. (1995) *English Gypsies and State Politics.* Hertfordshire: University of Hertfordshire Press.
Mead, G. H. (1934a) *Mind, Self, and Society from the Standpoint of a Social Behaviourist.* Chicago: University of Chicago Press.
———. (1934b) "Mind, Self and Society," in Morris, C. W. (ed.) *The Philosophy of the Act.* Chicago: University of Chicago Press.
Meyer, A. (1954) *Marxism, the Unity of Theory and Practice.* Cambridge: Harvard University Press.
Miles, R. (1989) *Racism.* London: Routledge.
Miller, C. (1975) "American Rom and the Ideology of Defilement," in Rehfisch, F., (ed.). *Gypsies, Tinkers, and Other Travellers* 41–54. London: Academic Press Inc., Ltd.
Montagu, A., ed. (1968) *Culture: Man's Adaptive Dimension.* Oxford and New York: Oxford University Press, Inc.
———., ed. (1975) *Race and IQ.* New York: Oxford University Press, Inc.
———. (1997) *Man's Most Dangerous Myth: The Fallacy of Race.* Walnut Creek, California: AltaMira Press.

Mussolini, B. (1935) *Fascism: Political and Social Doctrine.* Rome: Ardita.
Munro, R. (1998) "Belonging on the Move: Market Rhetoric and the Future as Obligatory Passage." *Theory Culture and Society* 46 (2): 208–43.
Nando.net. (1996) "Mrs. Clinton Tells Gypsies Not to Give Up." Associated Press.
Nemeth, D. J. (2002) *The Gypsy-American: An Ethnogeographic Study.* Lewiston: Edwin Mellen Press.
Noonan, P. (1994a) "Policy-Making and Travellers in Northern Ireland," in McCann, M., O'Siochain, S., and Ruane, J., (eds.). *Irish Travellers: Culture and Ethnicity.* Belfast: Institute of Irish Studies, Queens University Belfast.
O'Baoill, D. P. (1994) "Travellers' Cant: Language or Register," in McCann, M., O'Siochain, S., and Ruane, J., (eds.). *Irish Travellers: Culture and Ethnicity.* Belfast: Institute of Irish Studies, Queens University Belfast.
O'Connell, J. (1994) "Ethnicity and Irish Travellers," in McCann, M., O'Siochain, S., and Ruane, J., (eds.). *Irish Travellers: Culture and Ethnicity,* 110–20. Belfast: Institute of Irish Studies, Queens University Belfast.
Okely, J. (1975) "Gypsies Travelling in Southern England," in Rehfisch, F. (ed.). *Gypsies, Tinkers, and Other Travellers,* 55–83. London: Academic Press Inc., Ltd.
———. (1983) *The Traveller Gypsies.* Cambridge: Cambridge University Press.
———. (1994) "An Anthropological Perspective on Irish Travellers," in McCann, M., O'Siochain, S., and Ruane, J., (eds.). *Irish Travellers: Culture and Ethnicity,* 1–19. Belfast: Institute of Irish Studies, Queens University Belfast.
O'Nions, H. (1995) "The Marginalisation of Gypsies." *Web Journal of Current Legal Issues.* London: Blackstone Press.
Oxford English Dictionary. (1999) New York: Oxford University Press.
Paine, J. (1937) *A History of East Harwich.* Vermont: Rutland.
Parkin, F. (1979) *Marxism and Class Theory.* London: Tavistock Publications Ltd.
Pico Della Mirandola, G. (1965) *On the Dignity of Man, On Being and the One Heptaplus.* Indianapolis, New York, Kansas City: Bobbs-Merrill Company, Inc.
Pitkin, T. M. (1975) *Keepers of the Gate: A History of Ellis Island.* New York: University Press.
Prigogine, I. (1980) *From Being to Becoming: Time and Complexity in the Physical Sciences.* San Francisco: W. H. Freeman and Company.

Rao, A. (1975) "Some Manus Conceptions and Attitudes," in Rehfisch, F. (ed.). *Gypsies, Tinkers, and Other Travellers*, 139–67. London: Academic Press Inc., Ltd.

Rehfisch, A. (1975) "Scottish Travellers or Tinkers," in Rehfisch, F. (ed.). *Gypsies, Tinkers, and Other Travellers*. London: Academic Press Inc., Ltd.

Renfrew, C. (1987) *Archaeology and Language. The Puzzle of Indo-European Origins*. London: Cape.

Salo, M. (1982) "Romnichel Economic and Social Organization in Urban New England, 1850–1930," in Salo, M., (ed.). "Urban Gypsies," special issue of *Urban Anthropology* 2(3/4): 273–313.

Sampson, A. (1997) *The Scholar Gypsy*. London: John Murray, Ltd.

Sandford, J. (1973) *Gypsies*. London: Martin Secker and Warburg Ltd.

Sarbin, T. R. (1986) *Narrative Psychology: The Storied Nature of Human Conduct*. London and Connecticut: Praeger.

Scheibe, K. E. (1986) "Self-Narratives and Adventure," in Sarbin, T. R., (ed.). *Narrative Psychology: The Storied Nature of Human Conduct*, 129–51. London and Connecticut: Praeger.

Schmalenbach, H. (1977) "Communion: A Sociological category," in Luschen, G., and Schmalenbach, H., (eds.). *Herman Schmalenbach on Society and Experience*, 64–125. Chicago: University of Chicago Press.

Schopenhauer, A. (1818) *A World as Will and Idea*. London: Routledge and Kegan Paul Ltd.

Shields, R. (1992) "Individuals, Consumption Cultures, and the Fate of Community," in Shields, R., (ed.). *Lifestyle Shopping: The State of Consumption*. London: Routledge.

Shoemaker, H. W. (1926) "The Language of the Pennsylvania German Gypsies." *American Speech* 1: 584–86.

Simson, W. (1865) *A History of the Gipsies*. London: Sampson, Low, Son and Marston.

Smith, A. E. (1971) *Colonists in Bondage*. New York: Norton Co.

Smith, M. G. (1971a) "Institutional and Political Conditions of Pluralism," in *Pluralism in Africa* 27–36. Berkeley: University of California Press.

———. (1971b) "Some Aspects of Violent and Non-Violent Political Change in Plural Societies: Political Change in White Settler Societies: The Possibility of Peaceful Democratization," in *Pluralism in Africa*, 153–65. Berkeley: University of California Press.

Sollors, W., ed. (1989) *The Invention of Ethnicity*. New York and Oxford: Oxford University Press.

Solomos, J. and Back, L. (1996) *Racism and Society*. Basingstoke, Hampshire: Macmillan Press Ltd.
Southwark Traveller Women's Group. (1992) *Moving Stories*. London: Traveller Education Team.
Spence, D. P. (1982) *Narrative Truth and Historical Truth: Meaning and Interpretation in Psychoanalysis*. New York: Norton.
Stepan, N. (1982) *The Idea of Race in Science: Great Britain 1800–1960*. London and Basingstoke: Macmillan Press Ltd.
Stewart, M. (1997) *The Time of the Gypsies*. Oxford: Westview Press.
Strauss, A., ed. (1964) *George Herbert Mead on Social Psychology*. Chicago: University of Chicago Press.
Sutherland, A. (1975) " The American Rom," in Rehfisch, F., (ed.). *Gypsies, Tinkers, and Other Travellers*, 15–38. London: Academic Press Inc., Ltd.
———. (1986) *Gypsies: The Hidden Americans*. Illinois: Waveland Press.
Sutton-Smith, B. (1986) "Children's Fiction Making," in Sarbin, T. R., (ed.). *Narrative Psychology: The Storied Nature of Human Conduct*, 67–90. Connecticut: Praeger.
Sway, M. (1988) *Familiar Strangers*. Urbana: University of Illinois Press.
Taylor, P. (1971) *The Distant Magnet: European Emigration to USA*. New York: Harper Torchbooks.
Thomas, W. I. (1971) *Old World Traits Transplanted*. London: Patterson Smith.
Tong, D., ed. (1998) *Gypsies: An Interdisciplinary Reader*. New York and London: Garland Publishing Inc.
Toulson, S. (1980) *The Drovers*. Aylesbury, Buckinghamshire: Shire.
Trigg, E. B. (1973) *Gypsy Demons and Divinities*. Secaucus.
van den Berghe, P. L. (1971) "Pluralism and the Polity: Theoretical Exploration," in *Pluralism in Africa*, 67–81. Berkeley: University of California Press.
Vaux de Foletier, F. (1970) "L' esclavage des Tsiganes dans les principautés danubiennes." *Etudes Tsiganes* 16 (2/3): 24–29.
Weber, M. (1922) *Economy and Society*. Vol. 1. Berkeley: University of California Press.
Willems, W. (1997) *In Search of the True Gypsy: From Enlightenment to Final Solution*. London: Frank Cass Publishers.
Woodward, K. (1997) "Concepts of Identity and Difference," in Woodward, K. (ed.). *Identity and Difference*, 29–30. London: Sage Publications Ltd.
Wray, M., and Newitz, A. (1997) *White Trash: Race and Class in America*. London: Routledge.

Wirth, L. (1964) "Urbanism as a Way of Life" (orig. pub. 1938), in Riess Jr., A. (ed.). *On Cities and Social Life: Selected Papers*, 60–83. Chicago: University of Chicago Press.

Yoors, J. (1967) *The Gypsies*. Illinois: Waveland Press, Inc.

Index

Acton, Thomas, 21, 27, 40, 47, 56, 58, 78, 109, 178
Adams, B., 22
American Gypsy, 5, 6, 10, 39–42, 46–47, 48, 55, 58, 60, 62, 69–72, 80, 84, 85–88, 89, 91; in California, 60; in southeastern United States, 11, 48–49, 93–95
Anderson, N., 173
Appiah, K. A., and A. Guttmann, 177
Axon, W., 74

Barking, East London, 1, 2
Barth, F., 62, 79, 109
Bauman, Z., 183
Beier, A. L., 74
Banton, B., 88, 101
Berthoff, R., 173
Biko, Steven, 96, 97
Boas, Franz, 25
Bonaparte, Napoleon, 71
Borrow, George, 40, 42, 174
British Gypsy Studies, 39–41, 43

Brown, I., 24, 34, 35, 40, 41, 69
Brown, Radcliffe, 25
Bruner, J., 7, 122–23, 124, 127
Bonny Downs, 1, 14
Burke Secondary Modern School, 136
Butchart, A., 17

Canning Town, 1, 37, 113
Chinese Exclusion Act, 84
Clarke, Nobby, 137
Clebert, J. P., 13, 21, 29, 34, 35, 41, 47, 57, 58, 79, 87
Clifford, J., 185–86
Cockney, 112
Coelho, A., 69, 71
Crabb, J., 80
Cromwell, Richard, 72

De Man, Paul, 111, 122
de Foletier, Vaux, 70, 71
Dublin Travellers Education and Development Group, 87
Dunn, R. S., 74

199

Durkheim, Emile, 25, 106
Dutch School, 41

Earle, F., 16, 86, 141
East London, 1, 11, 20, 98, 112, 113, 114
Entrikin, J. Nicholas, 174
Essex, 1, 11
exclusion, 102–104, 106–107, 108–109

Fanon, Frantz, 7, 96, 131, 135–36, 178; and colonial narrative, 138–40, 145
Flew, A., 123, 131
Fonseca, I., 29
Foucault, Michel, 8, 9, 16–17, 40, 147, 172,
Fraser, A., 8, 13, 21, 27, 28, 45, 55, 66, 142, 188
Freud, Sigmund, 126, 131

Geana, G., 42
Gilroy, Paul, 180
Grellmann, Heinrich, 174
Goffman, Erving, 119, 127
Goldberg, D. T., 169
Goldschmidt, W., 25
Gottingen University, 10
Gropper, R. C., 24, 35, 40, 42, 70, 90
Gutmann, A., 128, 177
Guy, W., 32, 178
Gypsy (Gypsies): behavioral phenomenon of, 40, 65; biology and, 3–4, 13, 59, 87, 180; colonialism and, 7, 135; East End and, 2, 11, 18–20, 114; ethnicity and, 4, 24, 36, 40, 65, 183; social forces/construction and, 14, 115; housing and, 16, 23; identity and, 3–6, 7, 9, 17, 18–20, 32, 35, 36, 52, 57, 65, 93, 96–97, 170, 175–76; social conditions and interactions and, 55, 58, 65, 183; white trash identity and, 18; intermarriages and, 32; itinerancy and, 30–31; language and, 5, 27–28; migration to United States and, 80–85, 88; narrative and, 115, 127–133; romanticism and, 5, 34, 178, 180; sea Gypsies, 54–55, 67; self-identification and, 5, 31–32, 64–65, 86–87; similarity to African pluralist societies and, 140–42, 145; traditions and rituals and, 2, 5, 26; youth work and, 18
Gypsy Lore Society (GLS), 188; Archives, 188

Hall, Stuart, 6, 96, 118–19, 174
Hancock, Ian, 6, 29, 35, 46, 56, 58, 59, 70, 74, 88, 89, 90, 95, 105, 107, 139, 147, 158
Handler, J., 74
Hawes, D., and B. Perez, 9, 30, 40, 57, 58–59, 106, 143, 178
Hetherington, K., 183
Hewitt, J. P., 111, 115
horse fairs: Horsmonden and, 11; Paddock Wood and, 23; Hoyland, J., and, 80

inclusion, 106
Irish Tinkers, 86
Irish Travelers, 11, 31; language and, 27

Jefferson, Thomas, 71
Jenkins, R., 33
Jones, S., 29

Journal of the Gypsy Lore Society.
See *Romani Studies*
Jusserand, J., 78

Kalaydjieva, 181–82
Kasler, D., 172
Katzman, D. M., 173
Kenrick D., and S. Bakewell, 21, 109
Kenrick D., and C. Clark, 59
Kent County, 11, 23
Kornblum, W., 29, 63, 64
Kuhn, F., 124, 175,
Kuper, A., and M. G. Smith, 8, 25, 140, 142

Lasch, Christopher, 183
Lee, W., 34
Liegeois, J. P., 21, 29, 30, 57, 58, 95, 99–100
Liverpool, University of, 188
Lockwood, W. G., 42
Lucassen, J., W. Willems, and A. Cottaar, 40, 45, 50, 52, 71, 170. *See also* Dutch School
Ludar, 188

MacRitchie, D., 73
Mandel, E., 78
Maffesoli, M., 183
Magee, B., 129, 130
Malik, K., 143
Marx, Karl, 17–18, 143
Marxism, 8, 143
Mayall, David, 41, 70
McCann, M., S. O'Siochain, and J. Ruane, 31
McCarthy, P., 21, 144
McNay, L., 8
Mead, George Herbert, 7, 111, 116, 133

McDonagh, M., 177
Mill, John Stuart, 185
Miller, C., 32, 62
Millwall Football Club, 137
Montagu, Ashley, 100, 110, 177, 184, 185
Montesquieu, 10
Movable Dwellings Bill, 187

National Gypsy Council, 86
National Origins Act, 84
Nemeth, D. J., 24, 31, 47, 50, 51, 78
Newham, 136
Nietzsche, F., 129, 130
Noonan, P., 87
Norway, 112, 113, 171

O'Baoill, Donall, 27
O'Connell, J., 170
O'Nions, H., 34, 170, 172
Okely, J., 23, 32, 41, 45, 58, 78, 79, 90, 95–96, 126, 132, 172, 174–75, 182
Orwell, George, 108

Paine, J., 69
Parkin, F., 7, 102, 104, 105, 106, 107, 108, 110, 172
Peddlers, 86
Perez. *See* Hawes
Pitkin, T. M., 88
Poplar, 2
Prigogine, I., 175

Rao, A., 33
Rehfisch, A., 33, 51, 143, 170
Rom, 3, 4, 46, 60, 188
Roma, 5, 52, 188
Romany, 3, 46, 86
Romani Studies, 71, 188
Romanichels, 46, 188

Salo, M., 42, 80
Sampson, A., 40
Sandford, J., 87
Sarbin, T. R., 7, 120–21, 122, 123
Sartre, Jean-Paul, 131, 172–73
Scheibe, K. E., 111, 127, 145
Schmalenbach, H., 183
Schopenhauer, A., 123, 131
Scot, Joane, 70
Scott Macfie Gypsy Collection, 188
Scottish Tinkers, 86
Shakespeare, W.: *Henry IV*, 78
Shoemaker, H. W., 71
Simson, W., 72
Sinti, 188
Smith, M. G., 141, 142. *See also* Kuper
Solomos J., and L. Back, 17
Southwark Traveller Women's Group, 43, 143
Spence, D. P., 125–126
Stepan, N., 100
Stewart, M., 40
Strauss, A., 115
Sutherland, Anne, 13, 24, 32, 35, 40, 42, 55, 60, 61
Sutton-Smith, B., 7, 111, 119
Sway, M., 24, 35, 40, 55, 70, 88, 89

symbolic interactionism, 7, 115–17

Taters, 171
Taylor, P., 89
Thomas, W. I., 173
Tinkers, 78, 86
Tong, D., 42
Toulson, S., 87
Townsend, Pete, 137
Transportation Act of 1718, 72; Gypsies to Australia and, 76–77
Traveler, 3, 4, 188

United States: hobos, 173. *See also* American Gypsies
universalism, 180

Van den Berghe, 142

Weber, M., 7, 101, 102, 110, 184
West Ham United Football Club, 2, 112, 137
Willems, Wim, 10, 29, 40, 41, 57, 63, 64, 65, 66, 71, 170, 171, 174, 175, 183, 187
Wirth, L., 183
Woodward, K., 101, 115
Wray M., and A. Newitz, 17, 18

About the Author

A renowned scholar and community leader, **Brian Belton**'s career is a product of his Gypsy and working-class background and growing up in the youth gang culture of London's East End in the 1970s, as well as his early career as a youth worker. Educated at Burke Secondary Modern School, his studies culminated in a doctoral degree from the University of Canterbury at Kent, which he believes was made possible by the endurance qualities that emerged from his early street-fighting career and a heritage of continued struggle against oppression and exploitation.

He is senior lecturer at the YMCA George Williams College in Canning Town, East London. Notorious for his innovative, inspirational, and challengingly radical lectures, he advances a message of equality that resonates with academics as well as the public at large. A prolific writer for both academic and popular audiences, he is author of a number of oral and sporting histories, including *The First and Last Englishmen, Days of Iron, Hammering Round, Founded on Iron,* and *Johnnie the One,* as well as scholarly works, including *Gypsy and Traveller Ethnicity* (forthcoming).